WOMEN, MINISTRY
and
THE CHURCH

WOMEN, MINISTRY
—*and*—
THE CHURCH

Joan Chittister, O.S.B.

paulist press *new york/ramsey*

 ACKNOWLEDGEMENT

The Publisher gratefully acknowledges the use of the following materials: "Brotherly Love In Today's Church" appeared in *America;* "Healing Language," "The Future of Religious Life," and "Ministry and Secularism" appeared in *New Catholic World;* "A Heritage That Empowers," published in *Sisters Today* (Oct. 1980), "Post-Conciliar Spirituality of American Benedictine Women," published in *The Continuing Quest for God,* and "Interdependence and Revitalization," published in *Sisters Today* (Nov. 1976) are all published by permission of Liturgical Press, Collegeville, Mn.; "The Sin of Silence—The Sounds of Care," is reprinted from *Peacemakers: Christian Voices From The New Abolitionist Movement* edited by Jim Wallis, published by Harper & Row, © 1983 by Sojourner.

Library of Congress
Catalog Card Number: 82-62418

ISBN: 0-8091-2528-5

Published by Paulist Press
545 Island Road, Ramsey, N.J. 07446

Printed and bound in the
United States of America

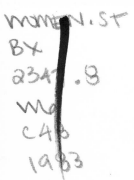

CONTENTS

CONTENTS

1. THE ROLE OF WOMEN IN THE CHURCH: PASTORAL VISION

If you're a woman, there is very little in the Catholic world that is new for women. Except talk, of course. There is a great deal of new talk. For instance, everyone is talking about women being "different but equal" and everyone is surely sincere. Most women and probably all men in the Church accept woman as different. It is simply difficult to find much proof of equality. Government is male. Business is male. The Church is certainly male. Those areas accepted as female—service positions and volunteer projects—are underpaid and undervalued. There is indeed a lot of talk, but unfortunately very little is actually done.

Why? The question is a nagging one but the explanations are even more troubling. The fact of the matter is that false biology and patriarchy—societies controlled by men with men's needs in mind—have joined to substantiate the secondary position of women. These circumstances, developed in detail in various historical studies, merit review for two reasons. In the first place it is the reality of the past and present out of which agendas must arise if they are to be more than an academic exercise or a venting of private anxieties. In the second place, the fact that these awarenesses have been common currency but unattended to for so long is itself part of the data.

The argument is not that earlier cultures consciously militated against women. On the contrary. Their lack of scientific information at least explains, if it does not completely validate, their social structures and mores.

The more serious problem is the fact that our generation, de-

1

spite scientific findings to the contrary, continues to operate as if woman by nature is inferior to man. As numerous scholars have attested, the primitive notion was that men were life-givers and women simply nourishing receptacles of the male seed in much the same manner that the farm land around them received the farmer's seed and brought forth a harvest. This notion has been theologized by every patriarchal religion since.

Medieval Roman Catholic Scholastics wove elaborate arguments to explain that man, by virtue of this life-giving potential, was spirit, reason and power "in the image of God" but that woman was carnal, emotional and passive. "Woman is secondary both in purpose (sex) and in material (body)," Thomas Aquinas said. "This has a negative effect on her moral discernment." Quite literally, then, man would have to be her head.

In the face of the nineteenth-century industrial revolution which completely separated the places of home and work, and Martin Luther's earlier insistence on the sanctity and nobility of marriage, Protestantism romanticized family life. Home and women became places apart from and not to be violated by the brutal male world. The final blow to the integration of women in society had finally been struck—and all in the name of religion and things spiritual. As a result, servanthood, subjugation and separation became not only an acceptable part of woman's state but necessary to her virtue.

The fact of the matter is that churches have sanctified the situation created by primitive misunderstanding, so it is the Church that must redeem it.

In the first place, an honest appraisal of Jesus' attitudes toward women, despite the rabbinical tradition of which he was a part, is clear proof of his own liberating presence, of his feminism.

Despite explicit Jewish laws to the contrary, Jesus treated women as full equals. He taught them, though the Jews denied women the right to study or discuss the Torah. He spoke to them in public though no Jewish man would even address his wife or mother or sister outside the home. He raised a woman to life again though women were seen as essentially unimportant creatures. He refused to stone the woman taken in adultery and so treated her as property as the law described. By healing the hemorrhaging woman who touched him, he rejected the taboo of primitive times which held that blood,

2

the seat of life and nourisher of the male seed, could not be spilled, as women did in menstruation, without incurring ritual uncleanness and expulsion from the sanctuary. He rejected the notion that women's place is only in the home when he afforded Mary the male right to discourse with the rabbis. He insisted on the same rights and responsibilities—monogamy and perpetuity—for both marriage partners despite the fact that in Judaism the man was permitted to put the wife away. He used, in the parable of the woman and the lost coin, a feminine image of God. And the apostles, aware of the revolutionary impact of these incidents, remarked on every one of them.

The point is that there is no Christian justification for the oppression of women. And now there is no biological, technological or psychological defense either. The explanation for the oppression of women, then, is that in the patriarchal society men own, control, shape and administer all facets of life, culture and society in such a way that the assumptions, beliefs and authorities of the group favor the males of the society. Men assume, for instance, that men should earn more than women, that men should receive more education, that men should lead, and that men are more creative or productive because it is men who have made the rules, written the texts, done the research, and conquered the territory to begin with. And after enough of that, everyone else begins to assume it, too.

In such a society the idea of man the planter of the life seed in passive soil, the important creator of life, and woman its spiller and defiler, is never far from the surface of the collective unconscious.

On those arguments the purification laws of the Jews and the churching ceremony of the Catholic Church were all based. Woman, unclean and unintelligent property, was denied education, confined to a territory, overruled by her masters, reduced to menial labor and denied liturgical exercise and participation in the community.

For centuries women have struggled against this denial of their full humanity with limited though significant success. Enough women have risen in every area whose abilities, character and creativity have been proof of the possibilities of the entire sex. But it is finally in this century that proof, possibility and potential have come together to challenge theologies that are at least un-Christian and more likely immoral. The discovery of biology, that women provide as many chromosomes to the embryo as males do, completely demolishes the supposition that man, more than woman, is lifegiver. The findings of psychology that women are as intellectually able, as emotionally balanced and as independence-oriented as men confront the notion that women are incapable of leadership, self-control and social perspective. The ideas become simply unfounded prejudice.

It is, then, out of the life of Jesus and the findings of modern science and the errors of past theological postures that this pastoral agenda on women arises. To be positive and just in its efforts to allow women the fullness of their humanity, the Church must, I believe, promote the following agenda:

1. *The Church Must Develop a New Theology of Family Life.* Parenthood and family security must be seen as the full responsibility of both partners. Mutuality that leads to the development of both persons—their talents, their interests, their joint needs—must be the basis of the marriage. Technology, family planning, child care methods and now even new modes of conception and fertilization demand that woman be defined beyond sex. She is no longer married to a house or confined by it. Marriage preparation courses that fail to take this very scientific liberation of women into account are preparation for nothing more than failure.

2. *The Church Must Come to Grips With Its Own Concept of Vocation.* It is the traditional teaching of the Church that there are three "states of life"—the married state, the religious state and the single state. If, indeed, all three are sanctifying, then all three should be available to both men and women. But women, faced with discrimination in hiring practices, wage scales, credit, and contract difficulties, are only barely able to support themselves or to function independently. If the Church is serious about promoting the dignity and equality of women, as well as the potentially sanctifying unmarried state, then it will have to promote civil legislation that makes this possible, speaking out in its behalf and calling for it. The Church, after all, supported the union movement and labor laws. Now another whole segment of the working population is struggling for survival.

The difference is that this time the sexism of religious tradition itself is basic to the problem. Unless the Church attends to this issue,

4

the conclusion must be that the assumption persists that women are to be dependent on men for their dignity and value.

3. *The Church Must Recognize Its Membership.* The language of the Church is almost exclusively male. The prayers of the Church only seldom acknowledge that women, too, are part of the congregation. The hymns sing of "brotherhood" and "fraternity" even when only women are in the Church. And, worse, the request to be included is trivialized as unimportant. "There are so many bigger things to be concerned about. Why waste time on this?" the argument goes. But history has a chilling answer. If women are the property of men, then of course there's no need to consider them distinctly. Who talks to John Smith and his raincoat? And if, as in the religious practices of the primitive tribes, only the males as direct descendants of the clan can dialogue with the ancestral gods, then clearly Christianity is only a male covenant. Jesus, however, led us to believe more. Paul confirmed it. And now growing numbers of women have come to claim their birthrights. Sexist language must go.

4. *The Church Must Authenticate the Ministries of Women.* For centuries the Church recognized the value and place of minor orders. Eventually, however, these ministries to the Christian community became consumed by the ordained priesthood. The re-emphasis on the lay vocation and the call to participation and community commitment by Vatican II of the entire Church as the people of God demands that the various gifts be identified and commissioned. Catechesis, social service, pastoral ministry, prayer and liturgy are all charisms of the faithful. And most of those ministries have been fulfilled over the centuries almost entirely by women. It is time to define and bless again all the services of Christian community so that both Church and priesthood can have full meaning.

5. *Women Must Be Given Roles in Decision-making in the Church.* Patriarchy and rampant clericalism have denied the Church its full measure of insight and ability. It is not possible to talk about ordination without also talking about power because the Church is run only by the ordained. The validity of the argument is attested to by the fact that as women have begun to seek ordination they have

been criticized for seeking power, an interesting accusation when you realize that men who seek priesthood are not credited with the same motives.

There is reason to believe, however, that the two factors—ordination and Church governance—ought actually to be separate issues. It is to just such division of roles that the Church must respond by giving women decision-making roles in the Church. Full membership in regard to parish boards, chancery offices, diocesan commissions, episcopal consultantships and sacred congregations is necessary if both women and men are to take seriously the Church's new admission of the equality of women.

6. *The Church Must Publish an Encyclical on Equality.* In order to lay to rest the theology of indirect redemption that has plagued the misunderstood humanity of women, it is time for the Church to speak plainly, boldly and clearly its acceptance of woman as a full human being. In a very special way, the woman's issue is the most radical of the justice issues. If the case can be made that one kind of human, the woman, is genetically inferior and disposed by nature to a state of subjugation, then domination is clearly part of the creative scheme. If women are less than men, so different as to be incompetent, so unreasonable as to be incapable, then it is a very short step to the justified napalming of Orientals, the lynching of blacks and the extermination of Indians because, it can be argued, the Creator God built inferiority right into the human race. An encyclical would give a fresh start to a Church ready for a new Epiphany and serve to soften or at least to balance the insults of earlier churchmen such as:

> Woman! you are the Devil's doorway. You have led astray one whom the Devil would not dare attack directly. It is your fault that the Son of God had to die; you should always go in mourning and rags. (Tertullian)

> Among all savage beasts none is found so harmful as woman. (John Chrysostom)

> Woman is an occasional and incomplete being . . . a misbegotten male. It is unchangeable that woman is destined to live under

6

man's influence and has no authority from her Lord. (Thomas Aquinas)

Woman is a sick she-ass . . . a hideous tapeworm . . . the advance post of hell. . . . (John Damascene)

Woman is slow in understanding and her unstable and naive mind renders her by way of natural weakness to the necessity of a strong hand in her husband. Her "use" is twofold: animal sex and motherhood. (Gregory)

So spoke the great men of the Church in the past over and over again. It is time for a Pope to speak otherwise.

7. *The Church Must Open the Diaconate to Women.* Deaconesses were a firm part of the tradition through the early centuries of the Church. The very fact that women are denied the privilege but men are not, now that the practice has been revived, is indicative of a basic and primitive and non-Christian attitude toward women. Unlike the question of priestly ordination, where sincere concern for tradition is at least a plausible question, the role of deaconess is well established and simply denied. In view of the rising consciousness of women and their manifest and continuing commitment to the ministry of Jesus, no pastoral agenda is complete without this question.

8. *The Church Must Revise Seminary Training Programs.* A negative attitude toward women has long colored the training of seminarians. Men who are supposed to counsel, confess and guide the spiritual development of women have historically been taught to fear them as the seducers and harassers of men, to expect mothering and submission, and to act paternal toward but not equal to women beyond them both in age and experience. That relationship is less tolerable every day.

Then, too, if the Church is serious in its commitment to involve women in the decision-making machinery of the Church it must also be willing to prepare them to accept it. That means that local seminaries should be offering courses in Canon Law, liturgy, Church administration and theology to women as well as to men who are interested in the pastoral service of the Church. It is certainly true that several large centers have already begun such programs. On the local level, though, little or nothing is being done to prepare clerics to work with women or women to work in the Church. Women are needed in these schools and on those faculties.

9. *Finally, the Church Must Attend to Its Educational Images.* What women are educated for or to has a great deal to do with their own self-images and the evangelical service they give. Passive virtues and private roles are not the stuff of equality. To define women by their sexual function is to seriously limit their full development in and for the kingdom. It is also to limit the development of men whose self-images, responsibilities and lives are skewed to the degree that women and their gifts are suppressed. The model and goals of women and men that the Church holds up as ideal will greatly affect the face of the Church in the future.

For a woman's agenda is not a woman's issue; it is a human issue. It is normally imperative, therefore, that women be all that they can be so that men are not less than they must be. In one of the Hasidic tales is embedded perhaps the crux of the question. The tale recounts:

> A certain zaddik died and soon after appeared in a dream to Rabbi Pinhas, who had been his friend. Rabbi Pinhas asked him: "What is the attitude toward the sins of youth?" "They are not taken seriously," said the dead man, "not if a man has atoned. But false piety—that is punished with great severity."

Sincere but false pieties have been the basis for women's inferior status throughout history; it is the kind of piety, baseless to content and evil in effect, that the Church must now confront if it is to grow to the fullness of Christ. And this demands that the Church educate to equality, raise women's expectations of themselves, and be a model for human justice. We cannot continue to separate roles and responsibilities on the basis of sex. We cannot define womanhood by motherhood unless we are also willing to define manhood by fatherhood. We cannot counsel people into bondage. Like the Canaanite woman, we come, agenda in hand, begging crumbs from the table of the master, not for ourselves but because our daughter has a demon. That faith made her whole. Any other piety will be severely punished.

2. "BROTHERLY" LOVE IN TODAY'S CHURCH

The Roman Catholic Church has a language problem. Shortly after "A Call to Action," the bishops' Detroit conference on liberty and justice, a newspaper in Cleveland polled its readership on the resolutions that came from the assembly. All the articles passed by large majorities—reinstatement of divorced Catholics, married clergy, total disarmament—with the exception of two that dealt with the position of women in the Church: the elimination of sexist language from Church documents and the ordination of female priests. These two failed. The losses were by slim percentages, but they were losses nevertheless.

Then, in January, the Vatican's Sacred Congregation on Doctrine published a declaration that reiterated the position that it is impossible for women to receive Roman Catholic priesthood. The same document, however, declared that "the real equality of the baptized ... is one of the great affirmations of Christianity," that "the roles [of male and female] are distinct and must not be confused" and that "woman's role is of capital importance ... for the rediscovery by believers of the true face of the Church."

But all the nice words are hard to take seriously. Unless the present language pattern of the Church changes, women cannot ever possibly become equal in it, or be identified as the true face of the Church, let alone become ordained to anything but an institutionalized recognition of their second-class status in the system.

It is my contention that the use of sexist language in the Church contributes to the continuance of a negative attitude toward women, affects the psychological development of women themselves, divides the Church, limits its resources and perpetuates injustice.

10

The history of the woman's movement can be traced through a number of social realities. Changes in marriage laws or customs through the centuries point to changes in the attitude toward women as human persons. Changes in voting laws indicate an acceptance of women as thinking persons. Changes in educational patterns have identified women as intelligent and creative persons. Changes in industry have made women co-creators of the environment in which they live. Women have come from being owned to being owners, from being kept to being keepers, from being led to being leaders.

But they have not come far enough, either in society or in the Church. In very few situations are their services valued to the same degree as those of the men with whom they work. Men get paid more for less certified contributions and have better opportunities for advancement. In very few instances is the presence of a woman really considered necessary to the project at hand, unless, of course, the task is a domestic one. In very few instances are their strengths noted and respected. Instead, they are, in most positions, tolerated and explained: "We got a woman because. . . . She's a woman but she's really good at. . . . We thought a woman might be able to get through to other women. . . ."

In the Church, women are barely permitted in the sanctuary, let alone allowed to preach or share the faith, regardless of their theological preparation. Even female organizations have been run or controlled by men. Laws pertaining to convents have always been written or approved by men and were much more stringent for women religious than for the male orders, so that women could be protected from their presumably weaker natures as well as from the environment around them.

Research in the behavioral sciences indicates that as a result of circumstances like these, women themselves, when tested, attribute more positive traits to men than to women. So poor is the cultural female self-concept, in other words, that women simply accept the notion that men are more fair, more intelligent, more capable and more effective than are women with identical experiences or backgrounds.

Progress has certainly been made. There are women in the federal government and on parish councils. There are women executives in both the ecclesial and civil structures. But at the very center of

11

cultural definition, women are not there at all. Women are excluded almost totally from language.

The Eskimos, anthropologists tell us, have eighteen different words in their language for "snow." Americans have at least that many for "car." Whatever is important to a group, in other words, is always reflected in its language. In the language of the Church, women do not exist at all. God comes to save "men," the texts say. We are all "sons" of God. We pray for the absent "brethren" and celebrate our "brotherhood" in Christ with "fraternal" joy. In the Mass prayers for the Sundays of Advent, as they appear in a missalette chosen at random, the Church refers to the congregation in some male form twenty-eight times. That count does not include a review of the Scripture passage or psalms. The hymns, to be sung also by women presumably, make an additional twenty references. Clearly, equality is not at issue here, nor is the face of the Church a picture of all its members.

Language shapes thought and attitudes. Theorists have questioned for years whether thought follows language or language follows thought, but oppressed people regularly point out the effect of terminology on acceptance and social rights. In the 1960's, leaders of the American Negro movement fought to eliminate "Negro" and the subservience the term implied, in favor of the concept that "black is beautiful." Today, feminists want to be called women rather than "the girls" or "the little wives." But to be called nothing at all, never even to be referred to directly at that ultimate moment of human community and dignity, the Mass, is even more devastating.

This failure of the Church to address women as women is effectively to make them non-persons who need not be dealt with. And if not at the Mass or, in the case of women religious whose breviaries are written and published by men, at the time of community prayer, then why would anyone feel it a natural thing to deal with them in the diocese or the parish or the Sacred Congregations?

The failure to name women in the same way in which men are identified in sacrament, liturgy and prayer simply overlooks half the Christian assembly. To pray in the assembly, it is necessary to be what you are not, or to be nothing at all. The most popular defense of the present practice is that the sexist terms "men," "brothers" and "sons" are simply generic, and that the issue is unimportant. In that case, two questions have to be asked: (1) Who decided which terms were generic? (2) Since it is not important, why not try it the other way for a while, since women are a majority of the population anyway? Let's pray, for example, that God came to save all women, that we are all daughters of God and that the Church should be a model of sisterly love. The change should be easy if it is really not important.

Clearly the consistent use of male vocabulary blurs the development of the female self-image in the Christian community. One of the factors that shape the human personality and self-image is the response to self that persons receive from others. By comparing ourselves to meaningful persons in our lives, we learn about ourselves. We come to define ourselves as too tall or a little short, as valuable or rejected, as intelligent or inadequate, by the way that others respond to our presence. It is the social "looking glass" that tells us who we are. Not to notice persons, not to reflect on their presence at all, is to communicate that they are unimportant, ineffective objects who are socially second-class. Women either do not exist at all in the hymns and texts of Church liturgy, or they are pictured as frail, weak and passive.

It is hard to make the case, then, that their presence on a few committees here and there is actually important to the Christian community. The question of who makes up the Church becomes a serious but subtle one. Women get included in its identity, but only generically, not as separate, dynamic contributors to its mission. Their importance becomes secondary. Who can read an ecclesial document or participate in Christian liturgy and really believe that women bring equal gifts to the building of the kingdom? What is worse, women themselves cannot possibly get that message clearly. Consequently, their life in the Church remains that of the weaker sex, the secondary role, the helpmate, the unimportant non-member.

As long as women continue to go unmentioned and uncalled, their presence as a responsible resource will also go unnoticed. Not only will the present generation lack a sense of woman's place in the Church, but future generations as well will likely find the intrusion of women into the theological and administrative arenas of the Church awkward and suspect, despite all theory to the contrary.

A great effort is being made to alter the vocabulary of children's textbooks so that girls and boys are identified separately. Until the Church does the same, it is unlikely that the next generation of male adults will be any more comfortable in sharing the mission of the Church with women than the present one. Unless recognized as strong, contributing, independent persons, women will continue to remain passive.

Social scientists repeatedly document the fact that because their self-esteem is low, women consistently give themselves and their own needs little priority. The gifts and vision and contributions that can be made by this part of the Church are therefore dependent on the self-image it nourishes in its female members. But to look at them and not to call them by name is hardly to build their self-image. As a result, half the resources of the Church fail to be highlighted, fail to be fully tapped. For all the men who believe that men are supposed to bear the ultimate responsibility for the other half of the human race, there are just as many women who assume it their natural lot to be disregarded or inferior or deprived. Unless women come into the language as valid and valuable members of the Church, the situation can only continue. This perpetuation of difference in human status and roles will ultimately weaken the Church as the secular society that surrounds it becomes more and more conscious of the equal dignity of the sexes and less and less tolerant of different valuations.

The point is that sexist language divides the Church against itself. Some men may not be conscious and some women may not care, but the fact remains that, in the language patterns of the Church, women as women do not exist. Cultures reflect in their language those things that affect their environment and have meaning in their lives. This is as true of the Church as it is of any other institution.

In fact, in its most recent declaration, "Women in the Ministerial Priesthood," the writers make a great point of St. Paul's word choice and build a case for the male priesthood on it. The text argues: "In the Pauline letters, exegetes of authority have noted a difference between two formulas used by the apostle: he writes indiscriminately 'my fellow workers' (Rom. 16:3; Phil. 4:2–3) when referring to men and women helping him in his apostolate in one way or another; but he reserves the title 'God's fellow workers' (1 Cor. 3:9, cf. 1 Thess. 3:2) to Apollos, Timothy and himself, thus designated because they are directly set apart for the apostolic ministry and the preaching of the word of God."

Then, without giving any explanation whatever, the writers refer repeatedly to the Church as "she" for whom the magisterium, male, makes decisions. Evidently, role stereotyping is an operative part of ecclesiastical communications and their meanings, and this at the very time that one committee after another has been set up to discuss women's rights and role in the Church. In the great effort to respond to this new consciousness, it is unfortunate that the Church has done little or nothing to dignify women in this simple but powerfully human way.

If the Church is indeed participative, if the Church is actually communal, then Church women as well as Church men must have a responsibility and an investment in its future. If all of us are the Church, then let us say who we are—the women and men, the sons and daughters, the persons of this Christian community—so that a baptized girl is as important and valued a member as a baptized boy. If not, then it is theologically imperative to rethink the whole concept of female baptism. Apparently, it differs from male baptism. How? Why? Someone has to ask the first questions. Someone has to demand the real answers. Someone has to question the assumptions. Who made them, and why?

From the point of view of structures, the fact that women are not addressed independently or directly in Church documents and rites divides the people of God in a way so deft that the discussion of the nature and place of women in Church and society is skewed from the outset. Until both groups are included equally in the language pattern itself, then the inclusion of women on boards, tribunals, congregations, theology faculties and pastoral ministries will remain a struggle and an oddity, a concept that is new or "experimental" and therefore suspect. Both groups have to be linked naturally in a basic perceptual framework before real equality can be achieved in administrative, economic and social structures. Otherwise, such positions of responsibility continue to be concessions rather than rights.

What is being proposed here is that a universal language be adopted for use in Church documents, rites, liturgies and hymnals rather than the generic terms that derive from male definitions and refer to all persons at once. To speak of "humankind" or "person-hood" is surely just as easy as referring only to "mankind" or "man-hood." In other places, it may be more loving and so much more appropriate to say directly that "we ask your blessing, Lord, on all women and men here and everywhere," or to sing that Jesus came for "them" instead of just for "men." No suggestion that male vocabulary or imagery be replaced by female language is even implied. To call God "she," it can be argued, is also sexist. To substitute one kind of chauvinism for the other is simply injustice under another guise.

What is proposed here is that men and women together approach the altar as equal persons. To pray with a group of men who are unaware that they completely disregard the presence of women in the life of the Church is disappointing. To pray with a group of women who are equally oblivious to that omission is to experience in the worst way the effect of the system on the self-image and ego strength of individuals who are consistently overlooked. To be willing to fill the role of non-person, not even to notice that it has been assumed, is certainly a prime example of the devastating effect of language on self-consciousness or feelings of self-worth and on the appreciation of one's own personal gifts.

Women religious, insofar as they have made a commitment to justice, have a special obligation to be models of justice, equality and presence for other women. At least in the convents of the world, women ought to be able to pray with their own identity.

But more important is the position taken by the official Church itself. The printing of hymns with sexist vocabulary can be stopped immediately. The use of prose that is actually indicative of only half the Church can be stopped immediately. There is no theological obstacle to the simple suggestion that male terminology be eliminated in favor of universalism or equivalence in address. If we are really serious about the role and value of women in the Church, then changing the language of the Church is an action that is tangible, achievable and without philosophical uncertainty. Bishops can change it; priest celebrants and preachers can change it; women can change it themselves for the sake of the growth of the Church and the dignity of other women; publishing houses can change it easily.

The psychological and social overtones of this simple gesture are manifold. Women themselves will grow in self-esteem. Men will become conscious of women's strong and special presence and be freed of false responsibility. The Church will become a model of justice in this area to all women of the world everywhere who are owned or exploited or oppressed.

The point is not that historical documents should be rewritten. Scriptural exegesis, translation and interpretation is a discipline that strives consistently to preserve historical accuracy and maintain relevance and meaning as well. As the understanding of the place of woman grows, these exegeses will take care of themselves. What is important at this time is not that old books or classic texts of scriptural revelation be altered, but that this Church now—talking to this Church now—talk to all of us so that all persons are dignified and included in the Church's understanding of itself. Either women do exist in this Church, or they do not. The language of the Church is clear and simple evidence of its answer to the implied question.

3. HEALING LANGUAGE

They were talking about things that healed and things that hurt the spirit. And one of them said, "Do you think it's harmful to eat some things?" And the other said back, "It isn't what goes into your mouth that matters; it's what comes out of it that can hurt." And nobody argued that at all.

When I was little they taught me to say, "Sticks and stones will break my bones but names will never hurt me." I knew even then that they were wrong. Words can hurt.

Human relations depend on communication. A long time before the divorce or the suicide or the career failure or the breakdown or the revolution ever happened, if anyone had wanted to do so badly enough, each of these could have been stopped. The hurt and pain, the damage and destruction could have been avoided, because each of those situations is, at its base, a problem in human relations. The point is that somewhere along the line the failure wasn't in personality or education or economics or feminism. The failure was in communication. Someone, somewhere said the wrong things or said nothing at all.

Or think of it this way: almost all mental health work—except in cases of organic brain damage from physical injury—is based on talk therapy. This means that words can heal as well as hurt.

Once we understand why language is so important it is possible to identify the kinds of language or communication patterns that have a negative effect on self-development, social interaction and mental health as well as to indicate which kinds of messages affirm and energize people.

Language tells us what everything is. Because of language we can distinguish and emphasize multiple variations of a single object—cedar and apple and willow as types of the thing "tree," for instance; skyscraper and condominium and hotel as kinds of public buildings. Because of language, in other words, we learn to see things in special ways. We learn to see what does or doesn't exist in our culture: eighteen kinds of snow if you're Eskimo; a dozen kinds of noodle if you're Italian; over thirty kinds of cars if you're from the United States.

But, more than that, because of language we learn to see ourselves. The messages we get from others tell us what kind of a person we're perceived to be: "a good little girl," an aunt said; "a sassy young thing," the neighbors said; "pudgy or sloppy or dependable or useless"; "a dumbhead, a smarty or a brain." In fact, we look to the reactions of others to discover what we're like, how valuable we are. We ask repeatedly, "Did you really think I played well?" "Do you really like my work?" Eventually we learn to see and define ourselves in these terms and as a result become more or less comfortable with who we are.

What is even more thought-provoking is the fact that it is this satisfaction with ourselves that determines the degree to which we can relate positively—healingly—to others, for our own value and goodness is exactly what we suppose and expect of everyone else. If we are dissatisfied with ourselves, if years of negative messages have told us only that we are somehow less adequate than other human beings, that we fail to measure up, it affects every human relationship we have for the worse.

Low self-esteem dwarfs the person we could really be. It sets false limits. It propels us through life looking over our shoulder to see what's wrong with us until, of course, eventually something is, even though we always wanted to be valuable and valued. This high ideal and low self-esteem finally combine to make us dependent on, but resentful toward, the direction and support of others, programmed to their expectations, and increasingly more burdened by our own lack of independence and self-direction.

Then someday all these hidden agendas—worthlessness, dependence, a mistrust of others based on the measuring stick that is our low trust of ourselves as persons—erupt into social reactions, often unspoken but never uncommunicated. The psychologist Gerald Egan says, "Feeling is never suppressed; it is translated into a number of ungrowthful activities." Hostility, resistance, passive-aggression and displacement of emotions are all simply manifestations of a communication system that is poisoned by a sense of personal inadequacy. Not positive about ourselves, we become defensive and hostile to others. Unhappy in our limitations, we nevertheless resist the influence of others. Unable to surface genuine disagreements for fear of further rejection or ridicule, we subvert the efforts of others or exert indirect control—by never being on time, for instance; by being slow and unresponsive at work; by forgetting or delaying or pouting. Unaccepting of ourselves as we are, unconfirmed in our own worth and unfree to be ourselves, we seethe over one situation in life but take it out on another—when the coffee is cold we kick the cat.

So the circle simply intensifies. The more poorly we relate to others the more negative responses we get back. And the negative feedback only confirms the basic unease we've had about ourselves ever since we began to accumulate those first sad signals: "fat, irresponsible, not as good a baby as her older sister."

Perhaps no incident is more telling than the research of E. R. Guthrie and its later replications. A psychology class conducted an exercise on low self-esteem by identifying an extremely withdrawn, unkempt, mediocre and unpopular student and reinforcing that person with positive communications about simple things. They said, for instance: "That color is perfect on you. Eileen said you're so easy and understanding to be with. We think that with your ability you're the natural person to chair the committee." Each remark was grounded on observable data, no matter how slight. By the end of the year, the student had joined several campus organizations, made the dean's list, become president of an important student group and created a social circle. Objective testing as well confirmed a rise in self-esteem and self-image. Obviously, the affirming attention of significant people had been a healing factor in the positive orientation of an otherwise colorless and even negative life.

Clearly, the effect of one human being on the development of another is profound. More profound is the fact that communication patterns, so unconsciously adopted, so casually explained away as "that's the way I am," are a basic part of personal growth, social effectiveness, and mental health. The important question is then to determine what kinds of messages obstruct full, positive development and what kinds of communication act as catalysts to growth. For it is the stunted individual, the person denied growth who is finally caught in the divorce, pressed to suicide, driven from the job, reduced to emotional distress, or frustrated to the point of revolution.

Kinds of Language That Hurt

A hurtful communication is any message that generalizes, devalues, or ignores the person. Each of these says "static" or "imperfect" or "bad."

1. *Labels and Stereotypes.* We know only as much about our world as we're able to perceive or consciously to acknowledge. But perception is affected by the language we use to describe what we see. For instance, to call a car a Rabbit or a Cutlass or a limousine is to shape perception, to include some characteristics of "car" but to exclude others. Consequently, language will alter our world vision. It does more than simply report. It draws attention to some qualities of a thing but not to others—even though a number of qualities are present in the same thing at the same time—and so influences our behavior and reactions. To call a stickpin a weapon is to emphasize a quality quite distinct from what we think of when we call it a piece of jewelry.

In other words, labels classify and categorize and evoke reactions that may have very little to do with the entire reality. Whole segments of society have been deprived and smothered in their personal development because people accept labels—Polack, ex-con, nun, woman, homosexual, retard—as a substitute for understanding the whole person. Many have never been able to grow beyond these half-truths.

Labels cut off communication and come laden down with negative vibrations that start the circle of self-hatred and social conflict. The point is that it hurts not to be allowed to be your whole self, your best self, but to be named and discarded for only a part of you.

2. *Evaluations.* After fifteen years of marriage it ceases to be funny that "she burned the first piece of toast we ever had and hasn't improved since." The not-a-good-cook mark translates so easily to not-a-good-wife and affects every other area of that self-image. In fact, always to be graded either good or bad in anything makes all of

life one long track meet, one great academic competition. The stress of being defined only as a winner or loser can eventually become the greatest burden of them all. To evaluate rather than to describe another person's behavior—"You're a drunk" instead of "You had six martinis"; "Jimmy's dumb" instead of "Jimmy got three C's and a D"—is the worst kind of entrapment. To get three C's is a fact that may change. To be dumb is a condition that is terminal. Even winners would like to be accepted for who they are instead of for the ribbons they've collected. Or, if not, what proof is there that the love will be there after there are no more ribbons to garner?

The point is that any evaluation, positive or negative, is a potential barrier to growth that hurts personal development and relationships as well.

3. *Evasions.* It is possible to talk to other people without ever really attending to them. And that may be the greatest put-down of them all. By interrupting, shifting topics abruptly, failing to respond to conversational leads or by giving minimal, unrelated or impertinent replies (uh huh; good, good; you bet) one idea comes through very clearly: neither you nor anything you say is interesting or important to me. Poor people report feeling that way when dealing with welfare agents. A woman's conversational topic, research shows, is hardly ever picked up on by men. The dead marriage, we know, is the one where even evaluations have given way to vapid, unmeaningful exchange.

Failing to attend to others in one way or another—failing to let them talk or ignoring their interests or responding without substance or meaning—is domineering and degrading. It is, furthermore, not communication at all. At best it is manipulation masking as interaction: what parents do to children; what bosses do to workers; what teachers do to students; what any powerful do to the powerless. It is the communication of unworth that hurts.

4. *Sexism.* But if evasion is bad, total non-recognition is worse. If someone says, "I'm so hot" there are four possible ways to respond.

1. Positively and directly: "Do you mind this heat?" or "Yes, it is warmer than yesterday," or "Heat can certainly make a difference."

2. Negatively but directly: "Don't complain about the heat," or "Heat is good for you."

3. Tangentially: "Your mail is on the table."

4. Not at all. Nothing degrades a person more than not even to notice that he or she is in your presence. It is a particularly hurtful insult. And half the human race is beginning to notice what a hurtful put-down it is to be treated as if they don't exist or are only owned by someone else. One half of the human race, women, are ignored or never responded to at all in the name of efficiency in language.

It is one thing to be an inferior or less important person. It is another thing to be no person at all. And that is the effect of sexist language: to subsume one entire body of people under the identity of the other, to absorb and deny their individuality, to snuff out their independent existence.

The argument against universalizing language (saying "people" for "men," for instance) is that male words include women too or that the issue is trivial. But words mean what people agree that they mean, and the existence of half the human race is not trivial, unless of course you really do not value it.

There is no such thing as the objective meaning of a word. Words connote whatever people think when they say them. Consequently, most meanings change over time. "Boy" has meant everything from "hangman" to "rascal" to "slave" to "young gentleman." When Chaucer used "harlot" it meant "good fellow." Once "Kleenex" and "Teflon" and "Victrola" were brand names; now they're substances, items. Obviously, words change in meaning when people begin to use them differently or look for new ways to express new understandings. Rockets, for instance, fly but were not called airplanes because that term is simply not able to draw attention to the distinctive characteristics of this new kind of flight.

Sexism is a language pattern that claims to recognize women but allows only male pronouns, terms, and so-called generic titles of male derivation (chair*man,* *brother*hood, *man*kind, fraternity). This non-recognition makes women essentially non-persons. No wonder that women become the unnamed property of someone else (Mrs. Charles W. Everett rather than Eileen Kelley-Everett). No wonder the Church can't hear itself talking only to men. A sacristan informed the new priest that the community preferred the use of universal language in the Mass ("humankind" or "all people" for "men," "community" for "brotherhood") and the benign, patronizing answer was "When I say 'men'—broad smile—I *mean* everyone." No more obvious a lack of concern for the dialogue of Eucharist or the existence of person can possibly be manifested. What the words meant to the female congregation were simply not important to him despite the fact that addressing someone directly or naming a thing gives them identification and therefore value.

A music publisher who refuses to edit sexist language out of hymn material, arguing that "the ERA is important but pronouns are not," is a person in the language business who doesn't understand language. What isn't in the language will never be in the culture or the mind. That women are not important enough to be recognized in the language is one reason why women don't have equal rights in civil law.

And sexist language affects the position of men in society, too. No word exists in the culture to describe the man who has fathered a child. She has "conceived," she is "pregnant." But isn't he part of it too? What has he done? What is he? The language doesn't tell us. Out of this exclusive linguistic attention to the biological process of bearing a child, the man's rights to child custody or the birth process have been almost obliterated. Only now are the courts beginning to grapple with rights of the unwed father, the divorced man.

New research attests to the general effects of this kind of nonrecognition on the self-esteem, personalities, success and emotional health of women.

The use of language to subsume or obliterate peoples is harmful to the development of the rights and responsibilities of both men and women. A great deal of healing needs to be done here.

So, what are the alternatives? What kinds of communication heal and bring to growth?

Kinds of Language That Heal

To be effective, language must be descriptive rather than evaluative, specific rather than general, responsive rather than ignoring, and open rather than defensive.

1. *Descriptive.* An antidote to the perils of evaluation is simply to state facts rather than to make sweeping judgments. If I'm a slob I'm socially undesirable and—since I am what I am—there's no hope. On the other hand, a descriptive message gives criteria for growth and a gauge to our relationship. Something like this, perhaps, gives direction in a way that the labels "gross," "dirty," "uncouth" do not: "I got caught in rush hour traffic three times this week because it took me extra time to pick up your clothes. Please do that for yourself so I'm not edgy about how the house looks or late for work."

No attack has been leveled, no vague expectations relayed. The contract is clear and the needs can be negotiated without a lowering of self-esteem or a denial of personal worth on either part. A message can be sent without name-calling that destroys the value of either person; growth thus becomes possible for both persons.

2. *Specific.* *This* car dealer, not *all* car dealers, has been dishonest. *This* woman, not women in general, cannot park her car. *That* motel, not the entire chain, is unsatisfactory. The ability to specify rather than to stereotype leaves us open to the possible value of every opportunity of life. Until absolutes and generalizations are eliminated from our vocabularies old barriers will continue to divide us as peoples and new insights can never emerge.

3. *Responsive.* Communication that fails to address, to recognize, to listen, to include is the language that separates groups into oppressors and oppressed. At the parish meeting, for instance, it is possible to say either "those people" or "some of us." One approach pits one group against another; the other commits all of us to work it out together. Instead of dividing people into camps by saying "*Those* people are agitating" or "*They* are never satisfied," language can be used to bring us together. We could say, "Some of us as citizens of the United States or members of the Church feel differently about things." But if it is "their" problem instead of "ours" then the lines are already drawn and revolution will be needed to resolve what dialogue could have healed to everyone's advantage.

4. *Open.* The impulse to evaluate, confirm or deny another's experience is an obstacle to communication. The need to agree or to disagree with another's experience (the "I-know-exactly-what-you-mean; why-when-I-was-there . . ." pattern) has often been considered

supportive. The fact of the matter is that support or understanding is not when you either agree or correct my feelings or experience but only when you accept the fact that they are my feelings and allow me to express them and to work them through with you. For it is that ability to admit and deal with my emotions and identity that finally heals.

Anything else blocks self-disclosure, the necessary basis of understanding and intimacy. It directs the person to tell us what we need to hear and so may suppress what the other person needs to say. As a result, people are less sharing, inclined to be wary of what they say, guarded in their openness and alert to defend themselves against rejection, ridicule, or reproof. People need to have their feelings accepted, their experiences noted, their equality and dignity respected. No put-downs, no hostile humor, no sermons are acceptable responses to the awesome truth of another human being's existence and effort to deal with life. Out of this respect grows trust and the possibility of a growthful relationship.

Clearly language can both hurt and heal. Why? Because language affects self-development, mental health, and social interaction. To be growth-producing, language must build self-esteem and personal worth. Language that minimizes others, excludes them, labels them, ridicules them is language that destroys the self, builds frustration and jeopardizes mental health. Language that attends to others as unique, trustworthy and worthy of respect contributes in the most humanizing way to the building of the kingdom.

The disciples wanted Jesus to say exactly which of the dietary laws were necessary to their religious development. But Jesus was not to be fooled by appearances. "It is not what goes into the mouth that saves," he said, "but what comes out that defiles."

And there is the secret of healing: To minister reverently to the other with the sacrament of language.

4. THE FUTURE OF RELIGIOUS LIFE

This is a bad news, good news presentation. The bad news is that the worst is not over for religious life. The good news is that the transition is at hand and may well be galvanizing for all of us. To get an idea of where religious life is going, however, it is important to understand where it has been and where it is now; that renewal is a process to be completed over time, not a project to be abandoned.

Psychologists have traced the life-cycle of human beings, biologists the life cycle of plants and animals, historians the life-cycle of movements and governments, and sociologists the life-cycle of groups and institutions. In every discipline the findings are clear: living things change as they grow, and each change brings with it a gift to be enjoyed and a task to be completed. But if that was common knowledge in the 1950's and 1960's, few watchers of religious life remembered to bell the cat. The result was profound shock in both the Roman Catholic population and in religious communities themselves as a life-style that had come to be seen as immutable began to shift and even apparently to crumble. For the most part, the changes were not generally seen as life-giving. And they were not easy. Nevertheless, religious life has apparently gone on. But why did it all happen? Where is it going now, if anyplace at all? Is religious life still a Gospel life or simply a paling shadow of a holier age? The question now is whether or not we are simply presiding over smoldering ruins or whether there is a phoenix in the ashes. It all depends.

The Development of Religious Life

The life-cycle of an institution has five major parts. In the period of *institutional origin* someone somehow senses the unspoken in society and proclaims it in the light of the Gospel. Mary Ward, for instance, sensed in her time that the Gospel would be unfulfilled until poor young women were educated; Mother McCauley sensed in her time that the Gospel would be unfulfilled until the sick were treated with dignity; Benedict of Nursia sensed in his time that the Gospel would be unfulfilled until the principles of Christian community were restored to society; Fr. Medaille sensed in another time that the Gospel would be unfulfilled until the common people of France were empowered through education to take their place in French society; Ignatius of Loyola sensed that the Gospel would be unfulfilled until the teachings of the Church were presented loud and clear; Mother Teresa senses in our time and her culture that the Gospel will be unfulfilled until the dying poor are treated as human beings and recalled to the conscience of society. At the period of origin, in other words, the institutional gift is awareness and the institutional task is concentration of resources. When the message is new and the revelation fresh, there is so much to be done and so many ways to do it. The group, impelled by the urgency of the call, has vision and energy. It often lacks resources and on-going leadership.

The second phase of the institutional life-cycle, if the group is able to concentrate its resources and consolidate its originating vision, is the period of *expansion.* In this period the group pours itself out like the widow's flour and oil: there seems to be no end to the needs to be addressed nor to the energy of the group addressing them. In this period, society too comes to recognize the founding vision and its own need for it. Schools and hospitals and orphanages, for instance, seem to spring up overnight, and everywhere. In the group itself, customs emerge which provide cohesion and economy of energy. The sense of mission is clear. The gift of this period is intensity and its task is to resist burn-out.

The third phase of institutional growth is the period of *stabilization.* The group, operating successfully now, begins to define itself and its operating structures. Life gets tidied up. The mission gets systematized. "We don't do that" and "We've always done it this way" get to be by-words. Rules begin to take the place of customs. The group becomes socially acceptable, part of the establishment, taken for granted. Everybody, including the members, forgets that this is the crowd that started in the countryside or the farmhouse or the streets. Respectability sets in. "Sister said . . ." and "Father wants . . ." become more social conventions and less prophetic insights. The gift is productivity; the task is to avoid activism.

But too often success punishes. Activism takes over and, with it, methodology. How a thing is done becomes much more important than what is being done. The ministry and structure of the group, in other words, begin to take pre-eminence over its initiating purpose and meaning. The vision wanes, even while the work flourishes. At the same time outsiders begin to see the group as just a bit anachronistic. Even the members begin to question why they're doing what they're doing. The old rules fail in their purpose. New possibilities, however, become unthinkable and energy fades. Nothing seems quite as important as it once did. The period of *breakdown* has begun. Morale drops; productivity deteriorates; membership starts to decline. Fewer people are attracted to the group; lifelong members begin to question its value; some even leave. The gift of the period of breakdown is warning; the task is transition. Vatican II called it "returning to the standards of the Gospel, the spirit of the founder, the needs of the members and the circumstances of the age." By the time Vatican Council II issued that mandate, though, almost one-fourth of all the religious in this country and others had already left religious life.

It is that past out of which the present and the future of religious life emerges. Clearly the period of transition is not an event; it is the process of a generation. And it is not inevitable.

The final phase of the institutional life-cycle, *transition,* confronts every exhausted group with three options: death, minimal survival, or renewal. Vatican II made renewal possible but it did not guarantee it. The decision rests with religious communities themselves, one at a time. Some will die—not dramatically, unfortunately. They will not, most of them, quit or say publicly that they have decided among themselves not to take new members, not to go on, not to try anything new, not to be Nicodemus people. Such a clear and simple sign that something must be done if we are to be able to go on responding to the will of God in this time as our founders and foundresses did in theirs seems unlikely. No, the fact of the matter is that most institutions die long before they cease to exist. The life goes out of them under the weight of the past and, eventually, they simply fade away. History is full of the phenomena. Over seventy-five percent of the religious orders founded before the year 1500 have ceased to exist. Over sixty-six percent of the religious communities founded before the year 1800 have died. Either they could not see through the filter of the Gospel the new needs of the world around them or they could not bear the effort it would take to stoop down to deal with them or they did not, in the face of old responsibilities, old debts and old ideas, anymore have the resources even to begin the shift. The important thing for this age to remember is that there is nothing wrong with death with dignity, provided that it is ringed with resignation, rather than with denial. In fact, this acknowledgement of services ended may be the last great gift these groups can give.

Some institutions at the breakdown stage, on the other hand, opt for minimal survival. They go through the motions of change but stop short of renewal. They plan an old Gospel game called new-wine-in-old-wineskins. They wear new clothes and take new jobs and say new words and form new committees. They're sincere and open. But they become sites instead of centers. Nobody knows exactly what they stand for as a group, nor do they. They may last but they will not lead; the prophetic character of religious life has passed them by.

Obviously, the gift of the period of transition is faith and its task is risk for the sake of the Gospel now. Renewal depends on it. That makes the present uncomfortable and the future insecure. It does not, however, make either period unhappy or unimportant. In fact, the present is exciting, not traumatic, and its future limitless, not grim. It is a period of beginning again with the mystery but without the mainstays of the past. Given these realities, what does religious life in this country at this time face in the future?

The Present Situation

Speculation about the future depends on an analysis of the present. We need to ask, then, what trends are developing now and what will the future look like if those trends continue.

Religious life is being buffeted by external as well as internal forces. It is not enough to simply say that old modes of community living have become outdated. Old schedules and old structures and old customs and old rules and old clothes are not the only problems faced by religious communities. If they were, then cosmetic changes would have been enough. As it is, whole charisms are still in the process of being retraced and retested because things have changed around, as well as within, communities.

First, in most cases and in most ways, the Gospel task of the last century which most communities set out to do has been completed. The children of the poor immigrant families from Europe have been educated and inserted into the culture around them. Medical facilities have been provided, even for the poor, by the state. The lay population of the Catholic community is, in most instances, capable of sustaining, staffing and even administering the Catholic school and hospital system themselves, not as free service to the poor perhaps as they were founded to do, but as an alternative system in a democratic society, an equally important but a nevertheless different kind of mission. Teaching and nursing, in other words, are no longer either the sole task of religious or this culture's fundamental human need. What we need now, then, is the gift of prophetic insight that characterizes the period of institutional origin if the Gospel is to be brought to this time.

Second, the Church has come to define itself as part of, rather than separate from, the culture around it. Consequently, it has rediscovered its role as leaven and salt rather than as city of God under siege, and this theology of transformation has touched religious communities as well. Many groups have relinquished a uniform or traditional religious habit in order to walk among people more like the Christ of Emmaus than the Christ of the transfiguration. They have opened their communities to non-members, become part of people's lives and made others part of theirs. They have found ministry outside of their own institutions and often outside of the Catholic structure itself.

Third, in the face of the arms race, exploitation by multinational corporations who pay small wages to reap unconscionable profits, the over-consumption of the Western world, and repressive governments, whole new pockets of poor and oppressed peoples have developed. There is a new Gospel agenda in our time for which old institutions are largely insufficient.

Fourth, like the culture around them, communities have aged.

People make life commitments at a later age these days and live longer after they do. Consequently, the average entrance age has changed from the late teens to the late twenties, not unlike either marriage or professional profiles. When people enter at that age, they do not come simply to do a certain work; they could obviously do any given work in any number of places. They come for a way of life, not for a way of working. They hold values for which independence is no substitute and which they apparently believe only religious life can fully support.

Implications for the Future

Out of all of these things is the stuff of the future. What can we expect to see if religious life is to be refounded in this century by these same communities who carried it and the Church with it through the last century? What shape will religious life take and what problems must communities expect to confront as they do it?

In the first place, there will be some obvious demographic differences. Religious communities will be smaller and older if for no other reason than the fact that the present replacement rate is slower and smaller than the growth rate of fifty years ago. That need not be a disadvantage to anyone. Older religious will be available to minister to older citizens, to pray with them, to speak for them, to mobilize them, to witness to the dignity of a group too long degraded by an economic system that made older people useless in order to control the labor force. What is more, the woman's movement will provide opportunities other than religious life for women who realize that marriage and motherhood are not their vocation. That in itself may affect the size of women's communities in the future.

In the second place, religious life will be less institutional if only because the institutions around which they have developed—large colleges, mammoth hospitals, and immense generalates—will themselves have shrunk or disappeared. This will affect life-style as well as ministry, relationships as well as work. Friendship communities rather than work communities will be more likely to form. Communal rather than individual spirituality may likely find more emphasis as well, when groups discover that since they do not form around common works anymore, they must form around something of more sustaining value than simply a common philosophy.

Third, new ministries must be developed, in the shell of the old if necessary. And time is wasting. It is no longer true in this society that anyone who wants a job can have one or that national security is guaranteed by national defense. Unless religious have gotten too professional to care for more than their own prestige, it is religious who must bring the Gospel to highlight these issues regardless of the cost to themselves. When that happens then religious life will be renewed.

Both the implications and the problems are clear.

Religious communities will make a conscious option for the future. Past structures and ministries are unalterably changed. Some communities will see in the Gospels a vision for the future that is not simply a memory of the past. If religious life is to both have and give the spiritual energy that these times need, in other words, it cannot be business as usual in the convents of the future.

Religious communities will be open to new ministries in behalf of a new set of people. Ministry arises out of the needs of the present, not out of the career preparation or successes of the past. There are new needs now. We have to start all over again with the same bias toward the poor of this generation as toward the poor of the last, with the same intent to see society from the point of view of those who are on the bottom of the social ladder this time as we are happy that we helped make possible the security of the last. At the same time, communities who have worked in one arena for over a hundred years are not able to move swiftly and totally to another as if they were indeed "without purse and staff." The buildings and debts and obligations of the past are in many cases with us still. Whole communities of religious cannot simply begin new works without support. In the future, then, we will begin to see more and more groups take corporate rather than institutional ministries, so that by common concentration on major important issues—peace, poverty, minority concerns, hunger and human rights—they may bring Gospel influence to bear on social development at large no matter what the individual works of their individual members.

We will begin to see more and more religious working for full salaries to support their communities so that more and more religious can work again for people who can pay nothing. In the near future, religious will work for stipends only where cause can be shown, not simply because part of the population has become accustomed to receiving free services from religious communities despite the fact that they are now able to pay, thanks to generations of religious before this one.

We will see community life and prayer begin to have new impact and take new forms. In fact, if community life and prayer do not begin to have new meaning, then it is unlikely that religious life will survive the transition from conformity and concentration on single works to pluralism and the call to individual giftedness within a common charism. Because the canonical homogenization of all religious into a standard brand vocation diminished both the character and the gifts of the various orders and congregations, that is no proof that fragmentation is a lesser evil. Like the Christian communities of Acts, religious need community and prayer not only as support but also as sign of the presence of Christ among them when the ministry is lonely and the direction is obscure. Multiple schedules, distance, and individual ministries will all militate against this, but effective communities will create new possibilities and members will make them a priority or it will not be long before communities become associations at best and signs of nothing at worst.

Functions will cease and functions will change. The woman's movement will have an effect on the kind of young women who come to religious life and the manner in which women religious relate to the rest of the Church and expect to be responded to as well. If women remain second-class citizens in a male Church, strong and independent young women of the future will not find religious life either a dignified or a life-giving place to be. That will shape religious communities themselves and the ministries they are able to provide for others.

Communities of male religious are faced with a role change as well. As the vocation of the laity develops and the clericalization of the Church is brought more and more into sound theological question, many male religious will have to discover a whole new quality of religious vocation that is just as crucial as any identity question that women religious have faced in the last decade and just as demanding.

Nevertheless, out of all of these circumstances can come a renewed religious life in which communities stand again for the word of God as did the prophets before them, in which action is no substitute for coming to know both God and self through prayer, in which community is indeed the Church in miniature and sign to a divided world that strangers can come together in Christ. In a study of long-lived utopian communities one researcher discovered that those groups who survived the most cultural changes over long periods of time were those who, whatever their structures or rules, held tight to six values: a basic and important belief system, community and sense of responsibility to one another, the renunciation of conflicting commitments outside the group, self-control, common ownership, and the willingness to sacrifice self for the sake of others. All of those elements are clear parts of contemporary religious life. Indeed there are signs of death in contemporary religious life—nostalgia, lack of response to present areas of need, individualism and privatism—but there are signs of life, too: openness, simplicity of life, faith, risk, a liturgical renewal, reckless unselfishness in the face of phenomenal demands and oppressive odds, and a growing awareness that it is the prophetic task of the religious not necessarily to staff but always to animate.

The fact of the matter is that we do not have a vocation crisis. We have a crisis of significance and spirituality.

The future will indeed be different, and the differences are necessary. If this generation of religious choose not to revive the vision, someone else surely will because the world needs these qualities as never before, and as Mary Ward, Mother McCauley, Benedict of Nursia, Fr. Medaille, Ignatius of Loyola and others knew before us, the Gospel will be unfulfilled in our time without them.

5. MINISTRY AND SECULARISM

It is assessment time. We are fifteen years beyond Vatican II and in this period massive social shifts have affected our life experience and our response to this experience. The changes of the last fifteen years, in fact, have barely settled yet. Some concepts have indeed clarified and brought new energy to community life, but other adaptations and adjustments seem, at least at first view, to be spinning out of touch with Church, community and sane institutional development. And of all the elements of religious life which bring wonder, concern and even condemnation of its present forms, ministry is the most central issue of all. It was all much clearer once: the work of the Church was to save souls and preserve the faith. As the great juggernaut of social change replaced small agricultural villages with massive urban settlements in a pluralistic world, it became astoundingly clear that souls were best saved and the faith most likely to be preserved in such a culture if the Church poured its energies into schools and social services, institutions that touched human development at its most significant personal moments. The Church, in other words, modeled the integration of the sacred and the secular long before secularism had ceased to be a threat for them. Religious orders, in a particular way, molded and pioneered these new ministries that were designed both to build and sustain Christian community.

In fact, eventually everybody began to take it all for granted—until recently.

There are new stirrings in religious communities. Some "works of the Church" that had been accepted as eternal have begun to be questioned and even to disappear. New involvements, once considered improper, or at least unimportant, are emerging to claim equal attention with standard ministries.

The tussle between the sacred and the secular has started again. Changes in ministry have brought tension, disorder and confusion. They have also brought, however, new energy, involvement and a sense of meaning. How are these very separate realities to be explained? Which factors are likely to prevail depends as much on the climate of the culture as the nature of the commitment. The questions to be asked are clear. First, are these new ministries legitimate expressions of living the Gospel? Then, where is it all going? Are there any present indicators to help us analyze what's happening now and what's likely to happen in the future? Third, how are these factors likely to relate to ingrained attitudes toward ministry?

For those that make a distinction between mission and ministry, the shift in forms of ministry is not as difficult to absorb and ministry becomes an easier concept to trace, type and predict. History is clear proof that what is happening today is not only tolerable but necessary, inevitable and basic to the mission of the Church.

The mission of the Church is, very simply, the proclamation of the good news by whatever means is intelligible and needed at the time. The mission of the Church is the announcement that Jesus is, saves, cares and calls us; that history is alive with the presence of God; that creation is purposeful; that the meaning of life is more than mere existence. It is a continuing message that must be constantly and consciously translated for every age (*Dogmatic Constitution on the Church,* par. 20).

Ministry on the other hand is the mode or manner in which this continuing proclamation is "manifested and preserved throughout the world." Ministries though will vary from culture to culture, from time to time, as signs of the saving, caring, calling Jesus present and made relevant to each living, dynamic moment of history (*Call to Life,* "Ministry").

The danger occurs when mission and ministry become confused. In that case people absolutize and petrify specific forms of service or witness and make particular works equivalent to the charisms which inspired them. In these cases, the power of the community to influence present circumstances is limited. The work of the group may go on but the questions of the present age will be hardly more than academic distractions. The community becomes dated. The community gets out of touch with the life questions of the age and so becomes unable to bring credible evidence to their resolution. Making ice cubes in Africa may be real proof of Christian love when the people are hot and thirsty. But if a glacier comes, then to continue that particular work is certainly to ignore the present reality if not to be downright silly in the name of religion. Though hard working, the community is largely ineffective. For some people surely, the continuation of refrigeration centers may be a sign of stability and traditional values. For many others, it will be only a signal that heat, fire, warmth, and care must be found elsewhere.

I am saying then, that ministry is mandated by the social climate of the time. I am saying, furthermore, that ministry is dependent on the economic structure of the period to make it possible to give it meaning and to make it effective. I am saying that it is Christian commitment itself, not a deluded secularism or selfish individualism that mandates changes in the ministry of the Church. The Church, in other words, leavens the system by modeling the system. And it has always been thus.

Once it becomes clear that the current economic system is the vehicle of ministry, direction becomes something that can be tested by more than intuition or personal interest. What I think is a good thing to do or what I think I'd like to do becomes, then, less the basis for choice than the fact that this good thing—which I am capable of doing with energy and commitment—is something that must be done at this period of time in this way if we are to be conscious co-creators of the kingdom.

The Western world has seen four stages of economic development: the agricultural period, the industrial society, the service-oriented economy, and, now, the post-industrial era. In each previous period, the ministries of the Church have been identified with whatever mode of influence was current at that time. Consequently, the key to understanding the changes in ministry now is to realize that the manner of social influence is changing once again. If ministry is to be as effective in a new world order as it has been in past periods, whole segments of Catholic service must change with it. What we will want Christians of the future to realize is that we were attempting to do that for this era by attending to the cares of this era in ways that make sense at this time, for the issues of this time cannot be addressed by the structures of a different world.

The Church and Land

When land was the basis for social influence, the Church had land. Up until the late Middle Ages the Church owned, administered and exercised civil control over vast areas of Europe. The papacy, bishops and large monasteries all maintained land for their own support, true, but also for the service of the poor. By collecting taxes or drawing income from large and lucrative benefices at a time when there was no public assistance of any kind, the Church was able to provide food, clothing and shelter for the destitute of the area. Land was the instrument of the Christian value system. Through its use of land the Church could lead, confront, leaven and call the entire social system to its obligations.

For centuries, the papacy struggled to hold and to enlarge the pontifical state, always aware that land was the basis of political and social leverage. The historian Coulton documents furthermore that the great monasteries of France, too, were real states. The Church was, then, at the heart of the social system, using it, shaping it to the profile of the Gospel. Through its use of land—the economic foundation of the era—the work of the Church was done in the way the people understood and needed most at that time.

In fact, if anything marks the Church as a failure in this period, it is that in some ways the Church neglected, misused, or resisted the social-economic structures of the time and so failed to be continually authentic in its proclamation. In very special ways, monastic manors were particularly slow or rigid in their adaptation to the needs of the serfs who worked their lands. Without doubt, religious communities owe justice to the circumstances of the age and will not be forgiven disinterest because they claim exemption from the agendas of the culture. Cluny, for instance, claimed the ministry of prayer in its thousand abbeys but was eventually destroyed for its failure to use the system to Christianize the system.

On the other hand, through the acceptance of entire kingdoms as vassals, the papacy provided protection, peace and security for whole nations. Belloc calls the Church of this period "the chief civil institution and the chief binding social force of the times" and the monasteries of the Dark Ages "the economic flywheels of those centuries."

To consider the Church and monasteries of these centuries a withdrawal Church is to repeat a romantic but unreal history. Through these civil systems the mission of the Church advanced, developed and permeated all of European society. To minister in this Church meant to be at the center of the system.

The Church and Labor

But then, with the Reformation and the industrial revolution, the social-economic situation changed drastically.

With the rise of industry and the drive for colonial development, social influence began to go to those who were able to amass and direct large forces. Land itself was no longer the measure of power or the tool of social change.

Like the society around it, the Church successfully adapted the economic character of the time to its own mission. It had, moreover, modeled a manner of dealing with large anonymous groups of workers in the new apostolic congregation without exploitation, disinterest or violence as Christian communities of service. The ministries that developed were clearly distinct from the monastic models of the earlier periods. Large numbers of religious—a veritable ecclesiastical labor force—moved from place to place at the direction of a single authority. The life-styles of the religious themselves were actually designed to be different. Some lived alone; they adopted military systems; they began to do specialized tasks.

In a labor-intense economy, in other words, the Church developed a labor force of religious to confront the circumstances of the age. As the people moved, the orders moved with them, mirroring their organizational patterns and mindful of their concerns. The Church too, had discovered the influence that came with the control of large groups of intense Christians who would transcend parochial and private interests in order to serve the needs of the universal Church.

Interestingly enough, the new group who arose to do these works were, at their inception, accepted only slowly, even by the

Church, because they didn't look or live as "religious" of the period were expected to.

But they thrived and the Church thrived with them until, out of this labor economy, arose the very factors that reshaped the major ministerial activities of the Church for the third time.

The Church and Service Institutions

The social effects of nineteenth century industrialization were as debilitating as they were exciting. Consumer goods increased; towns grew; the factory-system provided paid labor for large numbers of unskilled workers. But social conditions deteriorated in other ways. People lived in overcrowded, unsanitary conditions; children were uncared for or forced into mines and sweatshops for long, grueling hours; epidemics broke out; illiteracy made the hard-won civil rights of suffrage, equality and self-government impossible to secure.

By the nineteenth century, institutions designed to provide human services that had before this period of industrialization fallen entirely within the purview of the home became the responsibility of the commonwealth.

And in this service-oriented economy, the Church developed whole new forms of ministry. Well before local and state governments provided social services as a matter of course, new religious congregations in the Church arose to establish the hospitals, child-care facilities, schools, shelters, homes for the aged and welfare agencies which we now consider work "proper" to religious; sacred, not secular. In the nineteenth century, over six hundred new communities dedicated to the specific work of teaching alone sprang into existence. This provision of alternate institutions in pluralistic societies successfully adopted this new form of socio-economic influence to the witness of a caring Christ. But just as important to the analysis of what is happening in religious life today, perhaps, is the fact that in order to do this, these new communities too differed in purpose, preparation and professional involvements from the orders established before them. Many faced both public and ecclesiastical resistance as they struggled for recognition and acceptance. The Church fashioned rules to control their development in a pseudo-monastic fashion; society criticized their existence or sought to obstruct their

41

work by subjecting it to the approval of the state. In Boston, in fact, schools and convents were torched in an attempt to intimidate the nuns from their education of immigrant children.

Nevertheless, these congregations raised to professional competence the largest educational and social welfare system in the history of the Church. As the religious of the Church had once used the land and labor-oriented economies to extend the mission of the Church, they had now developed parallel service centers as the basis of a witness that was again both in but not of the culture.

Now, in 1980, one hundred and fifty years later, their influence undenied, their credibility established, these groups too are facing the displacement that comes with every shift in economic life and major social structures. For the basis of social influence is changing again and with it past forms of religious ministry.

A New Model of Ministry

In this post-industrial or technological-era land, labor and isolated institutions no longer count as the compelling forces of human life. For land, labor, institutions and even nations have long since ceased to be the binding social forces, the flywheels of society. International suprastructures, facilitated by instant communication networks, travel that is faster than sound, and computers that synthesize the data of decades in seconds make the entire world an interlocking system of related units. In this society, no single local person, no single local force either controls or shapes the life destiny of their given parts of the world. Worse, international economic associations which transcend national boundaries but affect every national interest answer to no one and touch us all. Marshall McLuhan's "world village"—an oblique metaphor fifteen years ago—is an overwhelming reality today as we watch millions die of starvation in Cambodia and find ourselves programmed by American computers that warn recklessly of nuclear attack from half a world away.

Obviously, in this world, it is not having ownership but having influence that counts. It is the decision-making process itself that bears attention and yields effect. It is to this ministry of influence, from the viewpoint of outer space, that the religious community has begun to turn. Political action, pastoral concerns, civil disobedience, social education, peace coalitions, advocacy positions, social justice platforms, and spirituality programs have begun to develop alongside the continuing but diminished institutional ministries of the first half of the century. As the world has moved away from localized institutional concerns, so have religious, so have the concerns of the Church. For this world faces issues that cannot be addressed simply by community programs, regional involvement and institutional ownership. The issues of equality, justice, peace, the distribution of world resources and human accountability stretch our commitments beyond and outside of ourselves. More than that, as the world's organizational patterns and agenda change with an evolving economic order, so do our own. It is to this new world order that we must continue to bring the model of the Gospel. But how? I suggest the following model of modern ministry.

In the new economic situation of this period it is necessary, I think, to make a clear distinction between *corporate* and *institutional* ministries. In this period of mass communication where success is measured not by what persons own or do but by the number of people who know their names, religious groups, like all the groups around them, must take their position in the arena of public influence. They must stand for something clear—speak for it, promote it, embody it—and network with other groups, if possible, to effect it. The group as group must identify a need, a question, an issue that is consonant with the community charism and then, as congregations and as individuals, work to make it possible.

At the same time, those institutions that are part of the community's past service system and still viable can continue under its auspices and philosophy as distinctly Christian and distinctly relevant. In this way, the community will indeed be doing something together that individual members cannot do alone; their institutions will still form part of their identity and purpose; they will be able to speak the Gospel in a powerful way to twin aspects of a culture that is both small towns and world village.

A new model of ministry, if it is to be realistic, must also include works that are both *direct* and *enabling*. For the fact of the matter is that in a money economy, barter and service are inadequate modes of maintenance. Religious of earlier eras did indeed serve for the bushel of potatoes it took to feed them or a gift of building materials, but that was long before gas heat, compulsory automobile insurance and state educational requirements.

Consequently, while some sisters continue to be directly involved in the defined works of the community or diocese, others will have to seek full-paying positions so that sisters can continue to maintain traditional programs or serve the new poor in now unestablished ways. It is the emergence of these positions which most often lead people to criticize religious for becoming "secular." But the fact is, if needed ministries are to emerge as they have in the past, some community members will give *direct* service to corporate or institutional ministries; others will have to provide the financial support to *enable* that for which no other sources—parochial or institutional—do.

Some facets of this model already exist almost everywhere. All of them are nowhere fully integrated and defined. But if purpose, focus and effect are to mark modern ministries as they have past situations, it seems that some balance of these communal, economic, and social realities must be achieved. Otherwise, the alternatives are bleak. The choice lies between (1) total commitment to past services, though sustaining these is difficult if not impossible as personnel and subsidies decline, or (2) the abandonment of all past institutions—even though these might still be necessary and desirable—in favor of positions that can sustain the community, or (3) continuation of the present practice of various commitments without common purpose and conscious focus—a possibility that must lead us to wonder how much effect this undirected approach can possibly have on the overwhelmingly complex circumstances of the present age.

Obstacles to Ministry

The social system is alive with new issues that cry to the Gospel for comment. Further the entire world has moved beyond parochial structures and local control to a world order that is transnational, interdependent and at the mercy of tightly controlled interlocking systems. In addition, the service institutions of the past century, once a major source of social influence, are, though important, declining both in numbers and in impact. What's more, the Church has always mirrored the structures of the time to address the questions of the time. Finally, ministers themselves feel compelled to move to new works, to new service.

All the elements are there to mandate a transitional model of ministry which, because it needs to have a foot in each culture, must be both corporate and institutional, direct and enabling at the same time.

But to move to Israel it is necessary to leave Egypt, as Moses found out with no less difficulty. The signs were all there, too: the manna, the quail, the cloud by day and the fire by night, the plagues and the call. But as Scripture clearly records, simply because God clearly wills something does not mean that it will be easy. There were obstacles, too: weariness, fear, idols, the Red Sea.

And, for us, this period is not without obstacles to ministry so basic that the whole direction—often painfully clear—seems just as often to be impossible. For deep within the same society that mandates movement there are obstacles so major that the transition may never be made.

The obstacles to transition as I see them at this point in history are, I believe, clericalism, institutionalism, intellectualism, fear of polarization, sexism, and secularism itself. These elements all affect the emergence of the lay vocation and the development of the ministries of women religious.

Clericalism. A pre-Vatican II Church, hierarchial by definition and structure, fostered for centuries the notion that the clergy were both central and superior members of the community. What's more, the attitude was sustained by culture as well as theology. Not only were some vocations defined as "higher" than others, but often only churchmen had the resources, the education or the social status to provide the leadership of an extremely localized society.

In the local parish priest converged every aspect of the society: the moral, the political, the economic and the communal dimensions of life. Unfortunately, that omniscient role expectation remained the residual norm long after the separation of Church and state, long after the compulsory education of the masses, long after the demise of self-contained communities, long after the rise of specialization.

As a result priesthood has become the criterion for liturgical participation, pastoral ministry, educational administration, diocesan organization, canonical lawmaking and general consultation in the

Church. The theological affirmation that God has given multiple gifts to all members of the Church for the upbuilding of the kingdom remains an aphorism but is yet to become a recognized reality.

With Vatican II and the call to the vocation of the laity, the trend can be seen for its full implications. For it is one thing to claim ministry by reason of ordination, but it is another thing not to claim it at all despite the mandate of baptism.

These two poles—clerical control and non-clerical involvement—come to sharp focus when persons such as the women religious of this generation see one form of ministry shifting and others, though open in theory, closed in fact. The adjustment to those who come to claim their birthright is commonly difficult for everyone involved. In this case, it may obstruct the development of ministry completely.

Institutionalism. Perhaps the greatest difficulty faced by the members of this generation of women religious is the success of the last. All over the United States large buildings, once used to house the large institutional ministries of the 1950's, now stand only half-full or in some cases completely empty. Many are still mortgaged. All of them cost more to operate. Most of them give high-quality Christian service that cannot be afforded even by the people who want it. Base populations are shifting. New disciplines make science studies more attractive than liberal arts and sophisticated technological equipment is difficult for small groups to finance. Curricula are expansive and costly, in other words. Government aid is slim or non-existent. Because of complex ownership patterns—parochial, diocesan, congregational—mergers are slow or impossible. How long every parish, community and diocese can continue to duplicate services in the name of Christian alternatives is a serious question.

In the case of religious orders it is often the fact that the identity of the group and its resources are tied into a good but currently untenable work. But since there is no going back, someone must go ahead as bridge-builders: to new kinds of ministry, to new populations, and in new ways so that we can be a Christian leaven when we can no longer be a labor force. But this time we must go as owners but not operators, as board-members but not staff-members, as directors but not as managers. Or else, when institutions end, so shall we.

Intellectualism. People who believe that religion is to be discussed but never to discomfit will not rest easily with a transition from institutional to social ministry. These people forget, when they say that sisters belong in convents and classrooms, that teaching immigrant children to take their place in an Anglo-Saxon, Protestant culture was once a very radical thing. Thomas Jefferson, for instance, did not really believe that commoners, females, and the poor should have the right to vote. Nor did many after him.

What religious did for the last generations—enable justice, equality, human dignity—we must somehow discover how to do again: first by determining to whom these are lacking and then by discovering how to press this system to provide it for them. For on such does the judgment of God, the co-creation of the kingdom depend.

Fear of Polarization. Some people would preach prudence to the crucifix. They worry so much that people aren't ready that they're willing to let other people's human rights wait forever. But sins against the Gospel in the name of unity are still sins. The fact of the matter is that it is its very differences, its polarizations since the time of Peter and Paul, that have made authentic the universality and the unity of the Church.

Indeed neither all the people nor all the Church is ready for a change in the image and forms of religious ministry. But what the people are ready for and what the signs of the times and the depth of the commitment demand have been different before. It is the history of the Church that every major adaptation in religious life has been met with resistance both from within and from outside the group. Unless we meet the needs knowing that neither the Church nor our communities will split unless we all agree to split them, then what we continue to call ministry may become simply a charade played with organizational finesse.

Sexism. Since the times that the world depended on brute force for security, since the centuries in which Aristotle and Thomas Aquinas defined the male as "reason" and the female as "carnal," women have been considered dangerous to a male's physical control, denied theological, educational and professional preparation, restricted from organizational participation and labeled emotional, incompetent, and dependent. The 1918 Code of Canon Law could group women with children and idiots without apology or explanation.

These labels linger still. Some people simply accept the inferiority of women as a fact; others over-react and claim for women a superiority of virtue, "purity," and status that is every bit as delimiting. From this point of view, women shouldn't sully themselves by getting involved with the mundane facets of life: politics, decision-making or public life.

The effects of these attitudes on the development of a ministry of social influence are obvious. To say that there are some Christian ministries that are limited by sex is to say that no one is obliged to the whole Gospel. Some demands of the Gospel are male, some female.

Sexism may well continue to obstruct the development of ministry in this period where the culture is reflecting new findings in the human and biological sciences more quickly than the Church which, for example, cannot even admit in its liturgical language that the Christian covenant is broader than the male identity

Secularism. Religious are committed to the good works of the Gospel. But the clear perception of exactly what those good works are is denied now by institutional decline and new social needs. As these factors touch them, as they attempt to adjust, they are pressed down, too, by the suspicion or accusations that their new works are not "religious," that they have become too secular.

The individual search for truth, the blurring of distinctions between the sacred and the secular, the tensions between transcendence and transfiguration, and the arguments of absolutes will certainly affect the identification of future ministries. But in the present moment, with traditional forms of service and charity on the turnstile of the times, it will not be, I believe, because religious do not do "appropriate" work that their ministry shrinks or that their essential commitment is clouded. Rather, religious who succumb to caretaking in the name of charity, rather than being an influence in the name of justice, will, in this new world, be the most secular of all. For it is the call to bring the foolish standards of the covenant to the issues of the time that is the mark of the ministers: Samuel, Deborah and Paul.

It is the poet Pope who writes, "To do the right thing for the wrong reason is the worst treason." It is *why* religious are wherever they are that will mark the value of their ministry now.

The move to new ministries may indeed undermine the spirituality of the past. Old schedules, rites and forms of communities have little to say to new questions, new demands and new life-styles. But without a loving faith-life and the call of Christian community, the best of ministries may simply drain the spirit dry.

Then, too, careers masquerading as ministries—works that may be related to personal development but not to the dangerous mission of the Gospel—will not long stand the scrutiny of call. In fact, many religious will have to give up good positions in order to call attention to the plight of the poor, to the callous lack of conscience of the system, and the corrupting effects of the search for "the good life."

Finally, only those works whose whole focus is to bring justice and individual dignity to people enslaved and exploited by greed will really stand the test of the Beatitudes. Any other works will be secular, no matter how standard their approval.

The Future

1. Basic changes in the social-economic patterns of the time imply that to be a Christian presence in the global village of the twenty-first century, religious must begin to give body to the ministry of social influence. If it is true that by the year 2000 only eight percent of the world population will be Catholic and only sixteen percent will be any kind of Christian at all, we must ask ourselves seriously what kind of sign we'll be.

2. In this transition time, it is our task to bear the institutional ministries of the past as far as they are viable, to build the social ministries of the future as much as we are able so that a new world order is not left without the goal of the Gospel at the center of its system, because religious and the Church have always been at the center before, bringing it testament, calling it on.

3. As communities of both the past and the future we must begin, then, to carve consciously ministries that are both corporate as well as institutional, enabling as well as direct. The co-creation of the kingdom—participation in the ministry of Jesus—is our call. But groups can give a kind of public witness and bring a kind of public

effectiveness that is not possible to most individual efforts. Consequently, we must as groups know who we are and what we stand for and then work together to achieve it in ways best suited to this time and culture.

4. Obstructions to ministry must be challenged at every point so that the courage of the past is honored and the kingdom of the future can come. For this generation will only be successful to the degree that the charism of the past is made capable.

5. Because the very social-economic bases of past ministries have evolved, there is no going back. There is moreover no standing still. The inability or unwillingness to move in ministry to the needs of the age is to choose to be quaint or comfortable rather than to be Christian. It is, in effect, to choose not to minister at all.

6. For in all of this, as opportunities for ministry change, as possibilities for ministry shift, it is not what is done but why it is done and the way it is done which will, ultimately, be the measure of its meaning. For the Christian the challenge is to bring to these new frontiers—to the heart of a complex social system—the simple dimensions of community, a contemplative integration of the spiritual and material, a hospitality that gives people warmth, space, the security to be, and the prophetic memory of Yahweh's terrible justice to the unjust.

It is a dangerous age.

To be a labor force is one thing. To be leaven is another. For prophecy, too, has its calls to compromise. In fact, the Hebrew Scriptures describe not one but four kinds of prophets, each of whom purported to proclaim the will of God.

The prophets of Baal were veritable whirling dervishes who, in a mechanical way, dedicated themselves to preserving a cult and performing a specific service. They claimed a relationship with God but were ineffective in their communication, mere window-dressing on the religion.

The prophets of the court existed to support the system. They spoke out, but were careful to say only what the king wanted to hear. Consequently, though they confirmed a lot of battle plans they also led a lot of kings to death.

The sons of the prophets were committed people whose intentions were good and whose sensitivities were sound. But they were full of fear. Determined to be safe and uncertain of their own energies on Yahweh's strength, they withdrew in bands outside the city to reflect and give witness. They never did any harm but they never did much great good either.

However, the real prophets of Yahweh had no private agendas—not piety, not institutionalism, not security. They were simply listening people who recognized a higher call to confront a present crisis. It was that consciousness that committed them.

They heard a message which they did not seek. They went places they never planned to go. They spoke things which often they themselves did not fully understand. They were rejected by the people to whom they spoke the message. And all of them suffered for the telling of it; all of them were accused of meddling in the secular.

But because of them, Israel survived. The promise became possible.

The real question of this age is a simple one: Are enough people able to hear? Are enough people willing to go? Both the quality of the past and the vitality of the future depend on it. Arguments about secularism may only be the ploy that makes the prophetic impossible in our time.

6. COMMITMENT TO COMMUNITY: BY WHAT STANDARDS AND WHY?

There are people who are still shocked, threatened or scandalized by the changes that have occurred in the life-style and ministries of religious in this last decade. And, though the concern is comforting, the anxiety may be misplaced. It was John Henry Newman who said, "To live is to change; to be perfect is to change often." It is history and sociology that confirm the fact.

Like every other living institution that emerges in response to social need and continues in existence because it continues to respond, religious life has adapted to at least five major moments in history.

In the early period of the Church, religious were hermits who left the pagan cities to witness to another life in Christ and to do battle with the devil in the desert.

When the Roman Empire fell, religious life became a model of Christian community.

When cities developed, religious went as itinerant mendicants to preach the Gospel and care for the poor.

Later, in the face of the effects of the Reformation and the Enlightenment, the dominant characteristic of religious was to be elite defenders of the faith who articulated the spiritual kingdom of the Church.

Finally, in the nineteenth century as a response to the rise of democratic societies and massive emigration patterns, the dominant paradigm of religious life became the missionary teacher. In this century over six hundred new congregations devoted exclusively to education emerged as the newest form of religious life.

In each of these periods, the cycle of origin, expansion, stabilization and decline led over varying periods of time to the need for adaptation and transition. In this decade we are dealing once again with the perilous process of institutional development. Vatican II and the advances of science and technology have altered our world views to such an extent that whole new responses are demanded.

But changes in community life are a necessary adjunct to changes in ministry. Consequently, though there are subjects other than community that make credible grist for any seminar on religious life, there is none more central, more perilous or more real at the present time. For what we offer as sign of Christian community may be the final measure of both our authenticity and our effectiveness. After all our prayers have been prayed and our work done, ultimately it may be what we are to one another that counts.

Two factors convince me of this: In the first place over two-thirds of the past members of religious communities questioned in one national research study attribute their decision to leave religious life not to problems of faith or celibacy or ministry or prayer but to inadequacies in their community life.

The group that responded indicated that they found religious life "lonely." Not stifling, not crowded, not exhausting, not superficial, but lonely. They felt, in other words, out of tune and out of sync with the community around them—unnoticed, lonely. Perhaps it means that no one cared about them. Perhaps it means that they didn't care about anyone else. But in groups that call themselves "religious communities" the syndrome is at least unsettling.

The second factor is cultural. This uncoupling of a group is a serious but certainly not a new problem. Individual families and groups have disintegrated before. People have felt tension, loneliness, insecurity, suppression and lack of mutual support since the beginning of time. But for the first time the situation has become a social malaise rather than simply a personal or local crisis. For some reason whole systems have begun to disintegrate. Whole peoples feel alienated and fractured. People sense, on the one hand, an empowering new kind of human community, and, on the other, the massive rupture of the human race. Never before has the joint sense of breakdown and breakthrough been so impelling. For the first time in history, human-kind has both the means of human unity and models of global inter-action. The technology of communication and transportation make the remote immediate. International collaboration enables us to monitor the weather, coordinate the mail system and upgrade inter-national medical care. At the same time, world resources are poorly distributed, pollution threatens the environment, whole nations of people are starving to death and ecological misuse in one part of the world affects the quality of life in another and the eventual survival of the planet. For the first time in history, the world is capable of its own annihilation.

The human community is in danger.

The religious community is creaking and groaning. Old forms of community life have been rejected. New forms have been found wanting.

For Benedictines with a fifteen hundred year tradition, the up-heaval has particular meaning. If you claim that "community" is ba-sic to your charism, but community is breaking up, then what is happening? What are its implications? For religious life? For you? For world development?

To treat this subject I believe it is necessary to deal with three questions: What has happened to community? What are the essential qualities of community? What is the function of religious community today?

1. *What Has Happened to Community?*

Unfortunately, many religious are tempted to believe that Vati-can II and the renewal of religious life created the problem. Before that, they argue, communities were united. After that, individualism ran rampant and past structures failed. I don't think so. I don't think that either Vatican II or individualism had much to do with the transformation of past models of community life. If Vatican II did anything at all, it simply acknowledged what had been going on for years. The problem is that, as the fairy tale implies, once the citizens admit that the emperor has no clothes, they are forced to deal with the fact. I don't think we changed community life; I think instead that it changed despite us and that we are the ones who must deal with the fact. Let us consider the important changes that have affected community over the centuries.

The agricultural model of community which lasted over seventeen hundred years was simple and direct. Community was related to place. Where people lived and with whom they lived determined their human relations as well as their life-support systems. Most people, Toffler says, never traveled more than fifteen miles away from home.

The impact of that reality, which incidentally was still true of the greater population as late as 1920, is overwhelming. It means that almost everything that people produced or used, every service they needed, everything they learned, every relationship they had, every activity that meant anything to them, came from the village and family in which they lived. Within those boundaries, in other words, everything that affected every person in the area took place. And they all did it together—all the time. Warren calls the self-sustaining society "horizontal community." It was cozy. It was clear. It was uniform. It was self-contained. Roles and relationships were very clear and very satisfying. They worked. Relationships were based on functions. Options were limited. Responsibilities were basic. And the cycle was endless repetition of survival exercises intent on insuring personal security and development through the interaction of the local group.

In that world convents and monasteries were simply mirror images of the social system. In fact, the Benedictine tradition sustained, modeled and organized that system in the period in which social structure and community first broke down through the disintegration of Roman civilization with its universal laws and controls.

Every monastery grew its own food, wrote its own laws, trained its own members, provided its own service, formed its own family and became the stabilizing factor which enabled people around it to do the same. Nothing else was needed; nothing else was wanted. On the contrary, that system brought order to the entire Western world for over fourteen hundred years.

It was centuries later that, little by little, railroads and communication systems, airlines and technology began to encroach on that world of self-contained societies, linking them, and interlocking them to one another. Now people could develop new relationships outside the group. Services became specialized and centralized; necessary products were formalized, provided, and regulated by outside agencies; government got bigger and bigger, and farther and farther away. Community, in other words, has become "vertical"—related in multiple ways to groups outside itself for all the facets of life: production, socialization, social control.

As people and things began to move great distances in great numbers, old homesteads and regions broke down. People lost the sense of local control and even local identification. Cities grew larger and larger. Houses were rented, not owned. Neighbors came and went with such frequency that the best psychological defense was not to get to know them. Home and work were separated by miles. People began to relate to multiple groups—to none of them totally, and to few of them deeply. The work group, the church group, the professional group, the family group, the club group were all different people in different parts and places of life. The psychiatric data of the last twenty-five years shows clearly that people began to feel less and less known, less and less cared about, less and less secure.

Nor were convents and monasteries exempt from the social upheaval. The new social dimensions of this vertical community began to touch us too. We began to buy the things we needed rather than to make them ourselves, to live away from our work, to be subject in our ministries to government regulations as well as to our own policies, to develop differing schedules and professional interests, to travel, to find ourselves also part of multiple institutions. We said we lived in one type of world, but we were actually coping with two, and the strain of trying to satisfy the demands of both was beginning to tell. People who lived in the most tightly structured groups in the country—religious—began to talk about being lonely.

In a rootless generation, community became the academic question of the day. Theologians, psychologists, sociologists, anthropologists, human relations experts and psychiatrists all began to see the need for it and to wonder what it was.

At the same period, Vatican II mandated religious to attend to the "signs of the times, the charism of the founder and the demands of the Gospel." Each of those elements too led to the question of community.

There can be no pretending any more. Someone has to face the question.

2. *What Are the Essential Qualities of Community?*

If community is no longer the relationship of people to place, then what is it? Is the old way possible at all anymore? And if not, what can take its place?

It is another sociologist, Rosabeth Moss Kantor, who provides the basis from which to explore those questions, I think. Kantor, like Warren, studied horizontal communities. In the midst of the commune movements of the 1960's, as alienated people by the thousands attempted to reclaim community by dropping out of the mainstream living pattern of nuclear families into extended friendship "families," Kantor began to analyze previous utopian societies to define their similarities, their differences, their longevity patterns. From that review of communal groups which had existed in the United States from 1780 to 1860, she drew comparisons of short- and long-lived groups in order to determine what qualities, if any, distinguished one set from another. Very simply, Kantor wanted to know whether communities that lasted a long period of time were significantly different in structures, values, or purpose from the groups that had disintegrated quickly. That analysis enabled her to report six elements common to long-term groups that were missing in large part in the shorter-lived societies. She calls those characteristics "commitment mechanisms" and considers them key to community development. What are those commitment mechanisms and what meaning, if any, can they have for religious communities today?

The utopian societies that lasted over a hundred years expected six things from their members.

First, they built their communities on the principle of *investment* or the concept that all personal profit must become the property of the group and irreversible: no property was privately owned; no back wages could be claimed if a person decided to leave the community. Whatever the person may have done for or contributed to the group stayed completely with the community for which it had been done. Consequently, leaving the group was clearly a major life decision and very costly.

Second, members were required to relinquish any *relationship* destructive to the group and to put group relationships first. Each group decided its own strategy for achieving this unity or differentiation. Some simply lived at a distance from other settlements. Others used titles or distinguishing clothing or activities to emphasize their common bonds and distance themselves from others. By whatever means, they made their obligations to the community primary, binding and conscious.

Third, successful utopian communities required *sacrifice* as a criterion for entry. In order to test the seriousness of the applicant's intentions, the group required that something be given up in return for the privilege or purpose of membership. This abstinence took many forms—alcohol, coffee, tea, tobacco, control of the sex life— but the effect was the same: the group itself was to be seen as more important to the individual's development than personal indulgence. Joining it was to be considered worth the loss of something else.

Fourth, members were expected to *mortify* themselves or, literally, to die to some part of themselves for the good of the group. By giving up complete autonomy, by focusing on the goals of the group, by being open to the guidance, needs and insights of other members, the individual began to know and own and live according to the ideals of the community. Being in the group was not a matter of personal convenience but a demanding way of life.

Fifth, in long-lasting groups, Kantor found *communion* or participation in group activities to be a basic priority. Common work, ritual and interaction built a sense of group togetherness and consciousness that heightened interdependence and the sense of corporate identity. Group members, in other words, were expected to know one another, to help one another, to practice life together.

Finally, every continuing community shared a common and meaningful *philosophy* or mystery or reason for its existence. Out of these came the tradition which they consciously maintained and the rationale for their existence. They were together for a purpose larger than their personal ambitions or survival.

If, as Kantor maintains, communities that embodied these six mechanisms lasted longer than communities that did not, what does that mean to me and thee in 1980, fifteen hundred years after Benedict and Scholastica, one hundred and twenty-five years after Boniface Wimmer and Benedicta Riepp, fifteen years after Vatican II, fifty years after a technological revolution that has changed the shape of human social patterns forever? What conclusions may we draw from these experiences about ourselves and the future of religious communities at this crossover moment in history?

In the first place, this comparison of secular, utopian groups is a clear indication that community is a quality of life, a set of priorities, an attitude of mind, not simply a set of "religious" behaviors or exercises which take place in a given territory. In fact, much if not all of the practices found in utopian communities are exactly the same ones which we so vehemently defended as essential to Roman Catholic religious life: dress, rank, abstinence, rituals, titles, distance. Strategies in every group were simply cultural and arbitrary vehicles of commitment and had nothing to do with its religious identity. The fact is that there is no such thing as a single style of community life. If the basic commitment mechanisms are consciously there, the cultural forms can always remain relative. To absolutize forms for their own sake and lose sight of the concepts themselves which inform or dictate them, as we did in the past, is to make institutional renewal traumatic, if not impossible. It is not what we do that makes community but why we do it. For the real essence of community is adherence to whatever type of investment, sacrifice, mortification, renunciation, communion and transcendence the nature of that particular group demands at any particular time.

Second, more broadly, the study indicates that commitment involves making the community a first priority, a guiding factor, a caring center in life. The physical, social and spiritual dimensions of community are not guaranteed by place alone and community can be achieved even if people do not always share the same space. But, of all the communities in a vertical world that a person can belong to, for real community to happen in a person's life, one of those communities must be given priority. We say things like: "Her family means more to her than her job." "His friends mean more to him than his family." "She doesn't feel that she belongs anywhere." We know when people commit themselves and when they do not. We know when we commit ourselves and when we do not. We know intuitively whether the criteria for commitment are real or imaginary. We know that community is not a refuge, a hotel, or an excuse for our existence. We know that community is a very active thing, not simply a daily schedule duly followed.

Third, community obviously demands some degree of physical presence. To call yourself a community member but never to bear the load, never to be with the others, to share their burdens, to touch their lives, to be open to their calls to growth is pure and utter nonsense. Telephone calls, Christmas visits and committee questionnaires are no substitute for doing the dishes, working at the festival, preparing the committee report, attending discussions, participating in the liturgy, or simply sharing the heat of the day. The point is that we can't claim cenobitic community and live outside it all the time. For, in the meantime, the community will go on without us. Community certainly demands the very physical dimensions of sacrifice and renunciation.

But, fourth, community demands social integration as well. Some people live in community and still live out of it. Some people bring their bodies to the group but never their hearts. They invest nothing and have communion with no one. They neither worry about anyone else's worries nor dream anyone else's dreams. They never love another sister or brother to life. In fact their anemic rigidity in the name of religion snuffs out both laughter and tears. Yes, they're there but they never trust; they never notice; they never pour themselves out. For them physical community is a mask for neurosis and an albatross in the environment. It is in this kind of passionless, conforming community that people get "lonely."

Finally, community also demands purpose and growth. For community to be community it must exist for something beyond itself or each of its members. Somehow, it has to mean something. Otherwise there's no reason to live together, no reason to listen and lift one another up. The group that ceases to ask itself why it is together is no community at all. Relationships, their quality and their meaning, are what community is all about. And that takes mortification and transcendence. It takes the discipline to live for something beyond ourselves.

It is to this balanced process of stable community building that I believe the Benedictine is called. That is the conversion, the *metanoia* of monastic life. It is, moreover, a process. Each of the elements may be absent in anybody's life at any given time and probably will be.

Participation, feeling, and meaning will all wax and wane between distance, independence, and uncertainty. Kantor found all the commitment mechanisms in few of the groups. In the more successful groups, however, she found greater recognition of the need for all of them. She also found that when more of the mechanisms declined at once, the more likely it was that the group would die at the same time. The important thing is simply that we not lose sight of the whole, that total community remain our vision. Anything else is only a plastic simile of the real thing that may, if we let it, trick us, too.

3. *What Is the Function of Religious Community Today?*

In the 1980's the obligation of a charism to community is awesome. Perhaps not since the chaos of the fifth century has a fragmented and turbulent world, a displaced and uprooted people needed the witness of Benedictine community so badly. This is no time to substitute stagnant rigidity for centers of life and love and growth. The world has seen enough of bureaucratic systems and numbing formalism and oppression. The world has seen enough of selfishness and exploitation and irresponsibility. The world needs to see the Gospel of love come alive in its own time.

For, I believe:

—It is the function of the stable Benedictine community to call the individual to growth. It is sharing life with a steady group of similarly committed people that enables us to recognize not their shortfalls but our own. It is their patient resilience that gives me both the temper and the time to stretch myself beyond my own impatience, narcissism, superficiality, unconcern for the meaning of the moment and the quality of the community itself. In the community around me, I can see clearly my own needs and the community's call for growth.

—It is the function of Benedictine community to exercise a corporate effect. Community enables us to do more together than any of us can do alone. It is the Christian community that can make the Gospel most credible in a Christ-less world. The Christian community does not exist for its own sake; the Christian community exists to prove that the kingdom can come.

—It is the function of Benedictine community to model the alternative possibilities of human life. If a community is authentic it can be a clear sign that simplicity, hospitality, obedience and celibacy extend, not diminish, the meaning of life. It is commitment to community through simplicity, hospitality, obedience and celibacy that gives prophetic proof that happiness is possible without the accumulation of goods, that in the kingdom of God there are no outcasts, that God is present and active in history, that strangers can become family in Christ.

—It is the function of Benedictine community to create a new vision of community. For the old community is over, but the new community is not yet formed. And when an old vision is clouded and a new one is unclear, people mourn the loss of their sense of purpose. Anomie sets in. Life loses energy and direction. People leave or live at a low level of involvement and a high level of anxiety; they break down physically or psychologically; they drift apart and the community dies long before it ceases to exist.

As Benedictines, we promise community. We tell the world—fractured by change, uprootedness, exploitation, and contact—to look to us and we'll show what community is. If that is the case, it is time for us to take ourselves very seriously. We need to look at our own communities physically, socially, spiritually. We must be more concerned about the quality of our relationships than the regularity of our schedules, the credits in our accounts, and the number of institutions we own. It is time to reach out, to speak for, to open ourselves to and enable others to build the human community as well.

Never since the fifth century has the gift of community been needed so badly. The question is: Can we—will we—give it again?

7. A HERITAGE THAT EMPOWERS

It is the function of a fifteen hundredth moment, I believe, to determine some place in my heart how I will know what are the new things and the old, to determine what are the pieties of the present time in an ancient tradition. My own answer to those questions depends on four things. I will share with you what I believe is: (1) the essential nature of a religious vocation, (2) the character of the present moment and its relationship to that nature, (3) the temper of the tradition itself, and (4) the obstacles we face in attempting to live that vocation at these times in that temper.

Let us look for a moment at the whole notion of vocation itself. What does our treasure of divine knowledge have to say to us about our obligations today? I think it is clear that the divine law is full of past models which reflect Yahweh's continuing expectations of those who profess to make a complete commitment. We can look back in the divine law and see that those who have answered the call before us have given us some clear criteria of our religious responsibilities. The religious vocation, I believe, is the vocation of Samuel, of Deborah, of Esther, of Paul.

I think that, like Samuel, those who claim to be chosen, those who claim to follow a call must be prepared to call another people to conscience. I believe that, like Deborah, those who commit themselves today must be willing to challenge a people to become their best selves. I believe it is of the essence of our religious vocation, like Esther, to risk our own lives for greater values. I believe, finally, that it is incumbent upon us, as it was on Paul, to change our own attitudes and through those personal changes the attitudes of whole other worlds. The function of the religious, these lives say to me, is to be loyal always to God alone, not to pay false debts to the past, and not to make systems the center of our lives. The function of the religious, I believe, is to bring the foolish standards of the Gospel to the issues of the age. Out of that perspective it will be easier to choose which new things and old, which pieties, because the problem of the age of renewal is not that we must choose good from evil. That would be easy. For committed people, choosing between good and evil is the touchstone of their lives. But the problem in a period of renewal is the responsibility of choosing good from good. It is unreal, irresponsible, and ridiculous to say that the past was wrong. The past was not wrong. The past brought us to this moment. The past was not only right, it was effective. The problem is that the past is past. But if the function of the religious is to bring the foolish standards of the Gospel to the issues of the age, we have to ask ourselves: What are the issues of the age, and what choices do we have?

Consider with me for a moment: As we sit here opening a new century, we are on the brink of the greatest ecumenical era in history. In Walter Buhlman's *The Coming of the Third Church* he states that if the present population and demographic trends continue, by the year 2000—in the lifetime of most of us—sixty percent of all the Christians in the world will live in the third world, in Latin America or Africa. But by the year 2000, given the present trends, only sixteen percent of the population of the world will be any kind of Christian at all. If we believe that our function is to be a sign of Christ, then we must take seriously the question: What kind of sign will we be?

Consider: As we sit here opening a new century, we are on the brink of a new world order. Let me illustrate. In 1775 at the beginning of our own country, two-thirds of the human race was dominated by the Western world; by 1945, at the end of World War II, half of the human race was still controlled by foreign forces. The United Nations was begun in that year and was planned and designed for seventy national states. By 1977 less than one percent of the human race was still under colonial government and there were one hundred and fifty-four nations in the U.N. Thus ninety-nine percent of the world's people had apparently achieved autonomy but not security, not dignity, and not development.

The consequence is a shift in the human agenda. We must now

be concerned with the agenda of the other half of the world. Any superficial reading of a newspaper in the last twenty-five years would prove that there is more stress now on the equity of all peoples, more stress on social interdependence, more stress on the human community and the common good. There is a lot less stress, or negative stress, on old institutions and goals now considered inadequate. Nobody is paying attention anymore to old values and their effects because they are now considered inappropriate. Very little attention is being paid to old centers of control and their needs because they are now understood to be oppressive.

Why the above? Because you and I, whether we want to be or not, are party to one of the four major transformations of the world: (1) the biological shift from prehominid to homo sapiens; (2) the social transformation: a shift from tribes to stratified society; (3) the technological transformation: a shift that moved nation states into a world village when for the first time in history, culture and ideas could spread worldwide instantly and economic and technological links were real; whether we want to or not, whether we are either willing or able, we are in our time about to face these consequences; (4) the ecological period of evolution: the transformation of society from intranational to true international civilization.

This new world is stressed not only by technology but also by space travel. From the perspective of outer space we now have a universal insight that we have never enjoyed before. We also have a sense of oppressive insignificance: What can I do about anything that is that much bigger than I am? In this new world view we are faced with exciting moments, but we are also faced with moments of cultural schizophrenia because, the anthropologists tell us, great moments of major transformation in any society bring both signs of breakthrough and symptoms of breakdown.

In this age, for instance, each of us or many of us born in the 1920's, 1930's, or even the early 1940's have felt the excitement of new possibilities. It is possible now, if we want to, to eradicate hunger; it is possible for us to unify the human race through communication; it is possible for us through world travel to respond to others' needs; it is possible for us to have global cooperation. We have examples (a) in malaria, in cancer research, (b) in information collection, and (c) in weather prediction and control. But our generation, too, has known the burden of breakdown. We are dealing with overpopulation which leads to serious hunger problems. Fifteen thousand people will die today as we go to supper; people will die from malnutrition, and the scientists tell us if the present trend continues by the year 2000 one-third more will die every day. Compounded with this we are facing serious and severe land loss in the world due to erosion, population, industry, abuse. By the year 2000 if things continue as they are, if nobody says stop, if nobody stands up and says no, we will lose one-third more of the land of the earth without conservation, without care, without reclamation, and without development. We also face the serious effect of air and water pollution in a planetary system that we have now discovered is unitary. For instance, the Amazon jungle supplies one-fourth of the oxygen supply for the entire earth. It is called the lungs of the world but nothing exists at the present time to stop the corporate mining and destruction of timber in the Amazon which is daily reducing the oxygen production of that area of the world. We are also living with the technological dangers that are symptoms of breakthrough. In Erie, Pennsylvania, we are ninety miles from Love Canal and one hundred miles from Three-Mile Island. The American Cancer Society told us last year that eighty percent of the cancers in this society are due to environmental and technical-scientific causes. Similarly, we are dealing with diminishing resources. Fossil fuels are limited but their usage increases daily. Worst of all, we are dealing with global illiteracy. Three years ago the United Nations tested teachers in American high schools on global literacy. At the same time they tested teachers in one hundred other countries. American teachers scoring one hundredth out of one hundred on that test indicated that they knew less about the globe, their own effects on it, and their relation to it than teachers in ninety-nine other countries in the world. Of course we cannot alert our citizens. In the face of all that, we support multinational corporations with budgets larger than most of the small nations of the world, and we do not have any international supra-structures whatsoever to require inter-nation accountability.

Consequently, in an age of massive awareness of massive maldistribution, one-third of the world's population (you and I) consume two-thirds of its resources and goods. Or think of it this way. Consider the world a village of one hundred people. Six of the people live in Western Europe and North America in a glass house where they eat and drink and wear and collect for themselves two-thirds of everything that is made in that village, while the other ninety-four sit on the lawn and watch. And it is getting intolerable to them. No wonder those six buy so many guns.

What is the point? We are at a fracture-point in history and we are its passover people. The psychiatrist, Viktor Frankl, says that, in the face of crisis, people will respond in one of three ways: (1) by denying the crisis ("Things don't look so bad to me. Look, I was in Nigeria and it looked pretty good; those people don't really want anything more"); (2) by despairing ("It's terrible. I'm part of it. I can't do anything. I don't know how to deal with this. I don't want to hear any more of this"); (3) by creating a conscious commitment to put themselves in a position of asking other people and themselves critical questions.

What does all that have to do with an anniversary? I think my only answer to that depends on the temper of the tradition as well as on the nature of the times. What is our proper response? What does the heritage really demand? The only way I can get into that is to look at the situation in the year 480, at the tradition's most pristine point, and ask myself: What kind of world did Benedict of Nursia face? I think this one: In 480 the superpower was declining. Order had broken down and protection had become impossible. All the standards on which people had learned to depend, all the securities that they thought they had, all the institutions that had worked before were now shifting, crumbling. As a result, too, the economy in the empire was deteriorating. Without the protection of the Roman legions, the roads were unsafe; farm land had been over-run; the production and marketing system had completely failed. Out of that they were faced with a tremendous social imbalance: a few rich; many, many poor; a few nobles, or decision-makers; most of them commoners and powerless. Exploitation was rampant. Slavery was taken for granted and considered "natural." There was social decay, of course: the distrust, the dislocation, and the destruction that went with this was everywhere. That was the world Benedict faced and he, too, had passover choices: (1) He could do what people said, "You've got to accept it. You've got to be real; that's the way things are. You've got to be sensible, do the best you can. Watch your own life and then, you know, other people will deal with those things." (2) He could run away: ("That's not my business. I'm a monk. That belongs to the Legion. That belongs to the imperati. All I can do, the best I can do, is just drop out.") (3) He himself could live a Gospel life. He could call others to that life. He could form others in it—a life that was orderly, productive, equal, common, meaningful, not destructive, not wasteful, not dominating, not competitive, not self-centered.

What's the situation in 1980? The superpowers are declining. Russia and the United States are tearing the world into two camps for their own ends. If we can get the Iranians to hate the Pakistani, the Pakistani to hate the Turks, then we can maintain all of the support and the economic lines that we have for ourselves. The economy is in turmoil. Consumerism absorbs us, even us. We live and listen to and let unchallenged the notion that the latest thing, the best things, and the most things have something to do with happiness. Whole peoples are exploited. Bananas that are picked in another country for five cents a bunch are sold in the supermarket in St. Cloud for $1.05. Women and minorities are underpaid; furthermore, they are defined as appendages to somebody else's achievements. They are denied access to any center that affects their own lives. Social bonds are deteriorating. Half of the marriages in this country reach the point of divorce. The ideal American family, the one that our second grade teacher told us all about—the one that shows up in pictures in the social studies books in the high schools: the mother at home, the working father and two children—makes up seven percent of the American population. If you include the definition to mean that the ideal American family is a working father, a working mother and less than two or more than two children, it makes up eleven percent of the American population. And relationships—people's warm, caring love for one another—have been lost in a metropolitan milieu. In a San Diego county last year, sixteen percent of the deaths in that county were dealt with by unmarked cars of strangers who took old bodies to crematoriums and then sent the ashes C.O.D. to their children someplace else in this country, and the sixteen percent were not the "winos," not the "alkies," not the addicts. In 1980 we face a tremendous amount of confusion and immorality. God has become a plastic statue, a fairytale figure. Pragmatism and the piety of law and ritual have replaced the social ethic.

If the question is "Is Benedictinism relevant?" my answer is: "Never more so." If the question is "Are we obliged to look at our world in a new and creative way?" my answer is: "We are every bit as much obliged as were Bede, Boniface, and Odilo; surely as much as Hilda, as Hildegarde, and Gertrude; certainly as much as a Boniface Wimmer and a Benedicta Riepp."

Benedict changed his society. Will someone tell me why we think we cannot change ours? The only false piety we need to fear, I think, is that this generation will be passive recipients of a very dynamic tradition. Our history is the history of a thousand new beginnings, and this is the time to begin again. This is not the time for monastic museums.

Though we want to find the power of the past for the future, though the social system is alive with new issues that certainly cry to Gospel Christians for comment, the crossover will not be easy. I promise you a crossover with great effort; it will not be without risk. To move to Israel necessitates first leaving Egypt (as Moses found out with no less difficulty). Moses had all the signs, too. Moses had to face the breakdown, the breakthrough moments. Moses and the chosen had manna for the hungry, quail for the restless, the cloud by day and fire by night, the plagues and the personal call. But Scripture records that simply because God clearly willed something did not mean that it was necessarily easy. In that passover moment in the desert there were obstacles too: weariness, fear, idols, official opposition, division in the camp, and the Red Sea. For us there are the same obstacles. The whole direction, often painfully clear, seems just as often painfully impossible.

What are our obstacles? What can we do about them? We are dealing, I think, with five obstacles to our response to present social issues which I have described as the identification of the new things and the old, and the choice of true pieties difficult and demanding but determinative. Unless these issues are faced by the Benedictines of this century, as courageous Benedictines of other centuries faced the social questions of the past, an empowering heritage will empower little or nothing in this day. For us to bring the foolish standards of the Gospel to the issues of the age it is necessary, I believe, for us to consider and confront these things:

1. We must confront intellectualism. Intellectualism is the no-

tion that the function of religion is to discuss but never to discomfit. Those who say that sisters and monks belong in choir stalls forget that their teaching activities, which are so totally and almost exclusively supported now, were once in this country considered to be very radical. Its purpose was to enable Catholic immigrants to take their place in an Anglo-Saxon, Protestant society, and for those efforts convents in Boston and Philadelphia were torched. Thomas Jefferson did not believe that commoners, females, and the poor should vote, nor did many people after him. What our founders and foundresses did threatened a whole system. It raised people to a dignity that enabled them to deal differently in a system which was designed to use them and not create them. I am trying to say that what Benedictines did for the last generations—enable justice, equality, human dignity through their schools—we must somehow discover how to do again: by determining to whom it is lacking now and by pressing systems, our own included, to provide it.

2. We must confront as well the problem of institutionalism. The greatest difficulty of this generation may well be the success of the last. I have a friend who says performance punishes. On the one hand we see population diminishing, our costs rising, our resources inadequate to enable us to go on where we have been. This will certainly make some previously flourishing institutions non-viable. In all honesty, in the integrity of the proper use of resources, certainly some of these must be and need to be closed or otherwise the energy and vision of our communities will be poured out on the road away from resurrection rather than toward it. Those closings are very difficult. In the process we are going to have to distinguish again between ministry and vocation. It is heartbreaking to hear sisters say, "But, Sister Joan, if the Academy closes, what will we do? Why would I stay a sister?" I submit that people who confuse their ministry with their vocation perhaps should have begun to examine that vocation years ago.

The function of a vocation is to be seized by Jesus, to have a relationship with Jesus, not to do a task. We will need in this process to learn new ways to serve, to bring that justice and equality, if we must, to close what is now not viable. We will need to ask ourselves continually: Can we animate or do we only staff?

But there is another concern about institutions that I consider even more serious. It is one thing, I think, for the institutions we own to be clearly not viable, but it is entirely another for them not to be prophetic. The gifting function of the Rule of Benedict is that it brings to consciousness the great questions of life: power, person, acquisition, community, union with God. Surely nothing that we touch should do less. Our schools, for instance, since they comprise the majority of our institutions, must educate, if we are keeping them now, for the issues of tomorrow, not for today. If we educate only for today, we are already behind. Concern for the here and now is a luxury we can no longer afford. Education for the here and now has left us with loss of energy supplies, with test-tube babies, with Three-Mile Island, and with less than equal rights for half the human race.

Any institution which we allow to exist today, in order to be Benedictine and prophetic, must focus, I think, on whether what is scientifically, socially, or economically possible is also humanly appropriate. Our institutions must be centers devoted to world peace, to equality, to social justice, to contemplation and reflection. There will be those, even our own, who press us, in a recession culture, to provide in our institutions only what is safe. "What will the bishop say? What will the benefactors do?" But we are once again in history in a wilderness where old answers do not work and where new answers can destroy.

In my opinion we can only justify those institutions which enable us to enable others to co-create with a contemplative vision and a highly critical clarity. Simply doing what others do is not enough; otherwise institutionalism will surely defeat us no matter how successful it seems. We are inheritors of a tradition that created an entire alternative society. Surely we can be as radical in the task.

3. We must confront, in the face of modern issues and their implications for the Church and ministry, the problem of clericalism. Clericalism is part of the Church's reaction to the Protestant Reformation. At that time, too, it was often culturally true that the priests were the only people with enough education or status to provide leadership. Consequently all parish roles began to converge in the priesthood. But a heightened theology of charism in Vatican II has affirmed repeatedly the gifts of this entire Christian community. Who will release them?

The concentration of ministry, authority, and leadership in ordination suppresses the rise of lay vocation. More than that, I believe that there may be residual effects that have never even been explored. I believe that the notion that there is only one leader or that authority is in only one person reinforces a sense of personal irresponsibility and diminishes people's gifts. It can lessen Christian accountability while we wait for the bishops, priests, and the officials of the Church to lead. But the Benedictine who has experienced cenobitic community knows we must all lead. We are all responsible. Benedictines come from centuries of lay communities. Surely we should be giving leadership in this area because it is so critical to the development of the Church. We must model that equality in developing ministry in our own communities. We should be enabling our sisters and our monks to develop the ministries for which they have been sent and to give the ministry with which they have been gifted.

4. I believe, finally, that we must confront the issue of sexism, the definition of Christian life that is based on gender alone. A recent Catholic sociological survey in this country published by the National Opinion Research Service indicates that in the United States one-half of all the women under fifty—wives and mothers, not women religious—reject the present feminine models offered in the official definition of the Church. The data shows, moreover, that two-thirds of the women under thirty are alienated from higher authorities of the Church because of rigid sex definitions. Women are beginning to wonder, in other words, if sex is basic to the Christian life, whether anyone is called to the entire Gospel; they are beginning to wonder whether or not those who do not have the full rights of baptism do or do not have its responsibilities either.

But "twinness" is basic to Benedictinism. Mutuality is the foundation of the era of dual monasteries. Independence and autonomy characterize the histories of male and female Benedictine communities. We are sitting in and at a major American model: two fantastically independent, creative, and flourishing communities who can live in the shadow of one another and both thrive. If no one else in the Church, at least Benedictines, both male and female, should be calling for and modeling equality in language and in liturgy, leadership positions of both women and men, and peer relationships in ministry for "in his own image" he made them both. We must do this—not for ourselves. It is too late for us. The function of our generation is to lay down our insights as a foundation for the next. Like the Canaanite women before us, "our daughters have a demon."

5. Finally we must confront the fear of polarization. Some people would preach prudence to the crucifix. In the face of controversial issues they worry so much that people will be upset because they are not equally ready and feeling good about the thing. But they are willing to let other people's human rights wait forever. Sins against the Gospel in the name of unity are still sins. Remember, on the dark days, that two thousand years ago nobody questioned slavery—not the disciples, not Paul. It was taken for granted; it was considered necessary; it was considered economically appropriate; it was considered natural ("Some people are born to be slaves"). But two hundred years ago, thanks to the questions of a creative minority, whole peoples have been brought to a fuller life.

From the time of Peter and Paul, the Church has known that tension does not have to divide; it can stretch and complete. From the Rule of Benedict we know that individual needs must be met. Benedictines commit themselves both to community and to the person, and we can show that communities do not split unless we all agree to split them. Things can be changed. But if we really want them changed, our own communities will have to allow people to begin. If we really are an Our Father people, if we pray daily "Thy kingdom come, thy will be done on earth as in heaven," then we must do something to bring it.

These issues, these frustrations indicate well, at least for me, what new things and old, what pieties will be acceptable on the other side. But if a religious vocation is to ask critical questions, if the function of a religious vocation is to bring the goad of the Gospel to the center of the system, if the function of a religious vocation is to call the conscience of the king, then the implications are clear. (1) It is the vow of conversion that is critical in our times. (2) We must risk new beginnings. We cannot sit and wait for people to be ready, for things to settle down, for letters to come, for constitutions to be written. (3) Faith is imperative. Courage is charismatic at this moment. I believe deeply that to be effective we must *choose* to be effective. Seventy-five percent of all the religious orders founded before the year 1500 are now extinct; sixty-six percent of all the religious orders founded before the year 1800 are now extinct. The survival of the religious life is not guaranteed by the approval of our constitutions by the Sacred Congregation of Religious. Survival is not guaranteed by virtue of good will. (4) The other implication is equally clear. Management will not be enough for these times. We have need for leaders now. (5) Despite criticism, despite opposition, despite rejection, despite censure, some of us must go on.

The role of religious in this world is to proclaim through their own love the presence of the caring Christ. It is to be living proof in a divided world that strangers can come together in Christ. It is to provoke consciences to the social standards of the Gospel, not to provide plastic statues for the fronts of people's cars, not to provide ritual or security. It is to be urgent in the upbuilding of the kingdom. It is to refuse to be satisfied with anything less than the ideals of Christ. It is indeed to empower the powerless, to stand with and speak for those who in their own quest for the dignity of creation must otherwise stand in this period alone. For it is the age again, I believe, of Samuel, of Deborah, of Esther, of Paul. It is a dangerous age. It is a time to begin again. To be a labor force is one thing; to be leaven is another, for prophecy, too, has its calls to compromise.

Note that Scripture describes not one kind of prophet, but four kinds of prophets. The first kind of prophets prominent in Scripture are the prophets of Baal. They were cultists, legalists. They did it rigorously well. They claimed to have a special relationship with God but they could never quite pay up. They were the window-dressing on the religion. The second kind of prophets were the prophets of the court. They existed to support the system. They spoke out but they were sensible, obedient. They said only what the king wanted to hear; they made a lot of kings feel good, but they led a lot of kings to death. The third kind of prophets were the sons of the prophets. Their intentions were extremely good and their sensitivities were sound, but they were very fearful and moved out of cities in groups to witness. They did no harm but they did very little good either.

The real prophets of Yahweh had no private agenda: not piety, not institutionalism, not security. The real prophets of Yahweh were simply listening people whose piety lay in recognizing that they had a higher call to confront the present crisis and that consciousness alone committed them. They heard a message that they had not sought. They went places they never planned to go. They spoke things that they themselves often did not fully understand. They were rejected by the people to whom they recalled Yahweh's message, and all of them suffered for the telling of it. But they would not be silent. Because of them Israel survived. Because of them the promise became possible.

As we begin another Benedictine century let us not live in awe of the past but in hope for the future. Augustine wrote: "Of the three theological virtues—faith, hope, and love—hope is the greatest. For faith only tells us that God is and love only tells us that God is good, but hope tells us that God will work his will." And then he writes: "And hope has two lovely daughters: anger and courage. Anger so that what must not be may not be; courage so that what should be can be."

As we participate this day and the rest of our lives in a heritage that empowers may the pieties of this period be anger and courage.

8. POST-CONCILIAR SPIRITUALITY OF AMERICAN BENEDICTINE WOMEN

The last decade in the lives of American Benedictine women has not been an easy one. In that period over twenty-five percent of the membership of the 1960's left religious life. After Vatican II some communities polarized or even divided over the ideological differences that had surfaced about the nature of the religious vocation. Both rising median ages and rising costs threatened the ministerial life of one group after another. Catholic schools and hospitals, once the focus of the sisters' active life, began to decline in the face of population shifts, government development of the public sector, and financial pressures. New ideas about the life-styles of religious confused the public and some of the sisters themselves. Criticism, conflict, and concern arose from every side. Vocations declined. It was an anxious time, a crucial time, an exciting time. Hope and fear walked hand in hand.

It was in this climate and by mandate from Rome that general chapters for the renewal of religious life were called. Women who lived a thirteenth-century life-style with twentieth-century responsibilities were being asked to integrate the two without overlooking the responsibilities or altering the essentials of the life. At least that's what all the documents said. I myself doubt that anyone really expected anything of them except business as usual. One less pleat here; one altered schedule there; a committee or two, perhaps. New wine but in old wineskins. It was when these women seriously began to ask themselves "What exactly are our responsibilities? What precisely is the essential character of the life to which we are committed?" that the depth of the conflict began to show. Layer after layer of behavioral custom and cultural accretions was peeled back in the search for the essence of the life. Nothing went unquestioned: the nature of obedience; the function of the vows; the composition of the community; the place of authority; the character of ministry; the charism of Benedictinism; the definition of community life; the place of religious life in the Church and society. One loose brick toppled the entire system.

The purpose of this presentation is to review the available data, not to explain the past—that has been attempted in detail by a number of related works—but to identify the priorities of the present and the concerns of the future.

At least six questions must be answered about the renewal movement among American Benedictine women in the 1970's if any positive influence is to be brought to its direction in the 1980's. (1) Will the present trends last? (2) What is the relationship of present expressions of renewal to the theories of renewal from the same period? (3) What has been resolved by renewal? (4) What new issues have emerged? (5) What are the implications? (6) What is the present character of religious life?

1. *Will the Present Trend Last?*

Preliminary to any talk about the future is the need to assess the present for signs of change or shifts of direction. In 1976 the one hundred and fifty-eight delegates to the five renewal chapters of a federation of American Benedictine women were asked to respond to a 453-item questionnaire. Of these, one hundred and forty-two or ninety percent of the delegates responded. This instrument was designed to assess their attitudes, behaviors, and beliefs about pre- and post-Vatican II religious life; to enable these delegates to describe their motives for change; to identify the pressures they felt then and now; to tap their feelings about what had happened to their religious lives; to collect their insights about present problems and future agendas. At the heart of the research was the unspoken question: If you had it to do over, would you do it differently? Are you sorry that you did it, now that you've seen what happened as a result? Chapter decisions ranged from ninety-five to one hundred percent consensus; very few could claim no responsibility.

Coupled to that question is its counterpart: Is this decade an aberration that will soon fade away, or is this new orientation deeply rooted and decisive for future direction?

The answer to those two questions lies in the relationship between attitudes, behaviors, and belief systems. Consequently, the research probed each aspect for consistency and depth of motivation.

The findings were clear:

—Though these women revealed in the attitude survey that they had been happy in their pre-Vatican II style of religious life, they also reported that they were much happier now and in many more dimensions. Pre-Vatican convent life they called "edifying" but associated it with a "static environment, dependency and immaturity." Post-Vatican life they did not call "stable, secure, or peaceful," but they did rate it "highly effective, hopeful, and meaningful." It is possible, however, for people to say one thing but do another. Therefore, the study had to determine whether the delegates' present behaviors were in harmony with what they claimed were their feelings. Did they confirm one kind of religious life but live another?

—We discovered in the second part of the study that not only did the delegates in a "paper-and-pencil forced-choice exercise" choose overwhelmingly for newly developed practices—traveling alone, discernment of ministry, elimination of the permission system, for instance—but they reflect these choices in their own life-styles. In a checklist response to current possibilities, they indicated that they themselves have indeed made major life changes in terms of what they do, how they dress, how they arrive at life decisions, how they function in community, and how they live the common life. The point is that this linkage of attitudes and new behaviors confirmed the authenticity of each. Women who were actually living a different life-style from the one they had been formed in for years claimed that it was indeed "sanctifying, positive, meaningful."

—Motives for change, furthermore, were rooted, they said, in newly internalized convictions that sprang from Church documents themselves with their new notions about the nature of Church and its place in the world, and not in external pressures. No one forced them to make changes in their life-styles. General chapters permitted adaptation; they did not prescribe it. Furthermore, no specific reference groups—friends, family, younger members of the community, priest advisors—seemed to weigh much at all in the delegates' final determination to restructure their community lives. On the contrary, the five factors that emerged as basic to their decisions to change were clearly remote from social pressure or control.

In the first place the group cited "the influence of Vatican Council II" and the documents that emanated from that body as fundamental to renewal. Since *Perfectae Caritatis,* the document for the renewal of religious life, did not deal with the relationship of religious to society, it was especially the Pastoral Constitution on the Church in the Modern World to which the chapter delegates turned for direction. It was the principles in these two documents that most reflected their own situation as active members of a monastic tradition.

From this understanding of the link between religious life and the Church came the second factor dominant in the chapter members' motivation to change the structures and forms of religious life as they had lived them in the past. They came, they said, to "new understandings about the nature of religious life."

On the basis of these theological insights and impelled by the direction of a Council, the highest authority in the Church, these women assessed their situations in priory chapters as well as in the meetings of federation delegates. Local communities, too, were disturbed by a growing consciousness of the elitism of religious life in the face of an increasingly egalitarian world and the model of the incarnated Christ. They grew convinced that the survival of religious life demanded real renewal, not simply reform, and made the last great gift of their lives: total risk. That local chapters launched experimental programs in almost every area of community life was a third factor, the delegates said, that led them to test and adopt change. Given their rejection of elitism and a concern for survival in the face of sudden and severe membership loss, the fourth and fifth most often cited factors, renewal was imperative. More, it sprang apparently from impulses that were deep and determinative.

If neither coercion nor the need for social approval is really at the base of the change in religious life, then its depth and longevity must be taken seriously. External pressures—force or peer group pressure—are commonly short-term factors: when the environment changes, the behaviors they prompted often do too. (For instance, children talk when the teacher leaves the room; people change their activities when they change friends or role models.) It is only behavior based on belief that is stable.

The basic question, then, is: Have sisters actually begun to believe something different about religious life? If so, what is it? What does that mean for religious life in the future?

If the delegates to these renewal chapters as opinion leaders, change agents, representatives, and officers of their communities are the reflections of their community populations, then indeed the philosophical base of contemporary religious life has shifted and will mark its forms and goals for years to come. The new ideas stand out clearly:

With a certainty that rings of the Church's own definition of the prophetic dimension of religious life, the research showed that the delegates believe that their ministries do not have to be designed or directed by the local institutional Church.

They also reject the notion that religious life is a special call to holiness or higher than any other vocation.

They do not believe, furthermore, that the essence of religious life is its separation from "the world."

They do not believe that the wearing of a habit is necessary as a sign of consecration and commitment.

At the same time, they do believe that religious life is simply Gospel life; that communities must be open and outgoing; that the witness of social concern through charity, simplicity, and compassion is a necessary part of their lives; that the quality of religious life depends in large part on the quality of the interpersonal relationships that are fostered there.

If these delegates are typical, we can assume that many religious do not believe in elitism and dependency and arbitrary prescriptions from outside their own experience. They have come instead to believe in personal growth and human relationships, the internal and independent authority of their communities, and a rich life with one another bonded by prayer.

From control, discipline, and suppression they have moved to value personal energy, life risk, and community, not as a laboratory of conformity or as an army of laborers, but as an environment for growth and love. This massive change in orientation will not be easily undone.

All the medieval manuals to the contrary, this generation has apparently truly come to claim the Gospels and not the customs books; the spirit rather than the legalisms of their tradition; the validity of their own experiences and the imperatives of the times.

In the face of this integration of attitudes, behaviors, motives, and beliefs, the present character of renewal in American communities of Benedictine women is hardly a fad. But is it representative of a cultural reality or simply a private moment in Benedictine history?

2. *Renewal Research and Theory: Gabriel Moran Revisited*

Concurrent with the early chapters of renewal were the writings of Gabriel Moran, F.S.C. and Maria Harris, C.S.J. on the survival of religious life in the United States in the mid-1960's. In the book *Experiences in Community,* they made specific evaluations of contemporary religious life and radical recommendations for change. Their point was that communities were coming undone, if not collapsing. Novitiates and scholasticates had virtually emptied out; traditionalists and reformers were choosing sides. The more structured or more repressive the groups, the more violent the upheaval seemed as education, experience, and new needs conspired against the traditional European ideal of religious life. Moran and Harris posited a need for "discontinuity," a "quantum leap" theory of change if religious life were to, or even should, survive.

Response to their work was electric. Disagreement was, in large part, emotional and unrelenting. Moran and Harris moved on to other projects and ideas, but the suppositions, analyses, and projections they left behind must be dealt with. Or else what is theory for? Were Moran and Harris unreal in their intuitions, or could many of us simply not hear them at that time? I have compared the survey findings of the national research done among Benedictine women in 1976–78 to the theses in the Moran-Harris work. Not every subject covered in their review was probed in our research, but a number of elements apply. In 1968 Moran and Harris critiqued the state of community life, ministry, obedience, and personal development in the religious communities of the 1960's.

About community life they argued that personal rather than task groups were essential to its witness value and growth dimensions. They maintained that its lack of warmth, trust, and love were dehumanizing what should be the most humanizing life of all—Christian communities of celibate and, therefore, universal love. They said that the quality of life would be improved if religious lived in smaller groups where personal relationships could develop rather than in large groups bound together by task alone.

About obedience Moran and Harris concluded that communal authority was more consonant with the Christian theology of person than the monarchical or bureaucratic structures that were presently at work in religious life. They said, too, that repression, especially in the personal events of life, was no form of obedience, and that freedom, rather than being contrary to doing the will of God, was basic to religious life. Participation and choice, they claimed, were central elements both to maturity and to religious life.

They reasoned further that if the *ministry of religious* was to be effective and authentic, it should be exempt from local ecclesiastical control. In order to pursue their responsibility to the universal mission of the Church, religious, they felt, should be able to develop without the constraint of diocesan systems or agendas.

They reasoned, too, that religious can and should work in non-Church positions and non-institutional ministries because the function of ministry is eschatological—to cooperate in bringing the kingdom of God now.

About the development of person they said some confounding and even more disturbing things. They said that the real revolution of the time was the new understanding of womanhood. Furthermore, they proposed that the ordination of women is essential to religious community and even to the real meaning of the priesthood as servant rather than status role.

Basic to all of these ideas and the general renewal of religious life itself, they felt, was not *Perfectae Caritatis,* the Decree on the Appropriate Renewal of Religious Life, but the Constitution on the Church, with its emphasis on openness, freedom of conscience, community, incarnation, and person.

These proposals of Moran and Harris shocked the religious community, angered many, depressed some. They stood for every-

thing that centuries of spirituality had decried and that the structures guarded against. Their critics argued that they offered, after all,
simply theory, perhaps even fantasy—at best, the unfaithful mean-
derings of a few.

3. *What Has Been Resolved by Renewal?*

Over a decade later, two separate research studies done among
American Benedictine women from coast to coast included similar
or related topics. What did these sisters believe about community,
ministry, obedience, and person in religious life after having changed
the structures of their lives so drastically? Did it support or deny the
Moran-Harris analysis of the religious environment a decade before?

Post-Vatican II community life, the respondents said, with its
elimination of formalized living patterns—controlled recreation,
specified association, lack of privacy, and denunciation of friendship—was now happier (88%), more loving (97%), more joyful
(87%), more supportive (86%), more developmental (97%).

Their notions of obedience had apparently been reformulated
too. Modes of decision-making had undergone vast change for over
three-fourths of the respondents. Their views were now sought, and
they had experienced an increased involvement in the creation of local community policy (80%). With two world-views in mind, the sisters said that authoritarian structures were unacceptable religious
practice (93%) and the right to take personal responsibility was imperative to spiritual growth (95%).

Their attitudes toward ministry were a sharp departure from
both their experience and their formation. They reported that changing needs in contemporary society called for a re-evaluation of community modes of service (80%). They claimed a heightened
awareness of social responsibility (98%), and some went so far as to
argue that a commitment to work for peace and justice should be a
criterion for the admission of candidates to religious profession
(60%).

They contended, too, that non-institutional ministries are a dynamic way to respond to current needs (82%) and that the best work
a religious community can do may well not be an institutionalized
corporate apostolate under the guidance of the hierarchy (93%).

About themselves as persons they began to offer some dangerous conclusions. Almost nine out of ten completely rejected the thesis of the Vatican document that men are clearer images of God than women are. Over half thought that women should be included on all decision-making bodies in the Church—national, diocesan, and curial. Almost two-thirds felt that they have an obligation to support the ordination of women.

Finally, as Moran and Harris claimed, the Constitution on the Church had greater influence on their decisions about renewal (80%) than did *Perfectae Caritatis.*

Clearly, the revolution that had been condemned as the unthinkable attack of an uncommitted minority had happened and was called good, satisfying, and hopeful.

But if these responses—one set from earlier renewal chapter delegates and the other from over sixteen hundred members of the Federation of St. Scholastica, over half of whom were more than sixty years of age—are any indication, the world may well have been too hard on Gabriel Moran and Maria Harris. Maybe we should have listened sooner, more lovingly, more thoughtfully, when there was still time to consider and prepare for the effects of all those directions. But now the dam is open. Is anyone prepared?

At any rate, it seems that just as the movement of the nineteenth-century Benedictines into missionary activities and, especially for Benedictine women, into the parochial school system was part of a wider social response, so is this current redirection part of a major cultural confluence that, through it all, retains a charism distinct for its emphasis on monastic community and liturgical prayer. But what has been the effect?

4. *Issues Old and New*

Formalism, depersonalization, dependency, institutionalism, elitism, and medievalism have been eliminated from sisters' lives in theory if not completely in fact. Most convents currently foster personal growth, creativity, and interpersonal development. The basic elements of the Benedictine charism—community, liturgy, ministry, contemplation, and hospitality—have been heightened beyond the levels of conformity and customs books.

But new issues press heavily, the respondents say.

Community: As works and schedules change, so does the whole structure of community life. Seldom is the large group together at one time; even small groups suffer the strain of individualized patterns. Whole new communication networks must be developed; new kinds of contact, new attempts to relate and respond, are needed. For unlike agricultural communities or even the educational period of the immediate past, doing the same work or having the same schedule can no longer substitute for a personally meaningful and richly spiritual environment.

Survival: Rising median ages, major financial pressures, and the decline of the traditional institutional works can threaten the energy, the focus, and the effectiveness of formerly thriving communities.

Schools close as population shifts. Small hospitals get crushed in the wake of technological advancement. Diocesan stipends fail to support even the maintenance costs of the average religious community, let alone provide the resources monies necessary if new works are to be undertaken, if retraining is necessary, if facilities need to be designed to meet the demands of the present rather than the once dynamic but now dwindling ministries of the past.

Ministry: The need to respond to new social issues is clear, but the means are limited. Sisters whose community roots are tied tightly into enfranchising the poor, the illiterate, and the social outcasts through education feel very keenly that their communities must respond again in behalf of oppressed peoples the world over. But how? With what? For most, it is by spreading themselves a little thinner, by taking people in, by networking in support groups, by encouraging some members to work at full salaries so that others can work for no salary at all.

But there are obstacles to the development of these new ministries. On the one hand, there are those who believe that teaching in a parochial school is an essential element of religious life. On the other hand, the IRS refuses to recognize both the concept of dependents and non-institutional ministry in the religious community and so taxes full-salaried, non-Church positions to the point that the ability to finance non-paying new ministries is greatly diminished.

The question is, then: Will the new shifts in ministry work and will they be enough?

5. *What Are the Implications?*

At the same time, women religious are steadfastly resisted in any ministry in the Church that is not connected with children or the sick. They may, of course, volunteer for some auxiliary services, but few are given official approbation for pastoral work, chancery work, or diocesan management positions.

If these limitations remain, women religious may have to leave the institutional service of the Church completely in order to develop vibrant community lives and a new network of private ministries. For business as usual is not the order of the day. Even more major risks will have to be taken as the commitment so characteristic of the contemporary religious is brought to new fulfillment. Old life patterns, old works, and old securities are all gone. It will take leadership like that attributed to pioneers and foundresses to enliven this crossover moment in history with the courage and the character to leave Egypt, because, as far as I can see, we too must go without escort, not knowing where we're going, but only whom we're following.

6. *The Present Character of Religious Life*

The research claims clearly that there is a new vision of religious life, but tensions still exist in communities as the old and new theologies clash. The old vision says that it is a function of religious life to be a state of perfection; the new vision says that religious life is, like any Christian vocation, a state of search: open, listening, changing, growing.

The old vision of religious life says that religious take vows to keep the law; the new vision says that religious take vows to gain life and give life.

The old vision says that it is a function of religious life to be a labor force, to do institutional work. But the new vision says that religious are not called to be a labor force but a leaven: a caring, calling presence that moves quickly into new needs.

The old vision says it is a function of religious life to take a stand *against* the things of the world; the new vision says that religious must stand *for* the things of the world—not *against* property, flesh, and will but *for* the poor, *for* justice, *for* love, *for* accountability, *for* a positive, not a negative, spirituality.

The old vision of religious life says that the function of the religious is to transcend the world, to withdraw from it; the new vision of religious life says its function is to transform it, to be in but not of it.

The research data show many Benedictine women following the illumination of the newer light. But if the two trends do not come to terms in the Church, the next decade, like the last one, will not be an easy one for religious.

9. ISSUES IN RENEWAL IN THE ROMAN CATHOLIC CHURCH

$\mathbf{A}$ttempting to treat a two thousand-year-old topic in such a short chapter demands that the treatment be necessarily simple. But some attention must be given to four elements if the reflection is to have any meaning at all:

1. What are the issues?
2. What are the turning points and tensions in each?
3. What is their internal congruence or relationship?
4. What are the implications of these issues for us as ecumenists?

It would surely be simple enough to define given questions in contemporary Roman Catholicism as issues in renewal. But it would be equally appropriate to question whether those were actually the issues of the Church or simply my personal concerns.

To avoid that dilemma I have chosen to identify as "renewal issues" only those concerns that were defined by the Church itself as its official renewal agenda—those topics dealt with by Vatican II itself and about which, as a result, separate declarations were written. Those sixteen documents addressed issues which the Council fathers obviously felt needed scrutiny and renewal in this period of the Church:

- The Nature of the Church
- The Nature of Revelation
- The Place of the Church in the Modern World

- The Nature of Liturgy
- The Place of Communications in Church Development
- Ecumenism
- The Status of the Eastern Catholic Church
- The Role of the Bishop
- Priestly Formation
- The Role of Priesthood
- The Renewal of Religious Life
- The Vocation of the Laity
- The Nature of Missionary Activity
- The Role of Christian Education
- The Relationship of the Church to Non-Christian Religions

My contention is that each of these topics is central to the renewal of the Church, that each generates or reflects a turning point in the traditional teaching, posture or direction of the Church and that each of them has introduced tension points which if unattended will be an obstacle both to real renewal and to the effectiveness of the Church as well.

Turning Points and Tensions

The Constitution on the Church

This landmark document embodies as its turning point the very definition of the Church itself. In pre-Vatican II Baltimore Catechism days, the definition was structural and straightforward. The Church, every child learned, was that body of lawfully baptized who accepted the tenets of the faith, were gathered about a local bishop and were in communion with Rome. Vatican II, on the other hand, enlarged the definition of Church beyond the institutional. The Church, the Council declared, is "the people of God." The focus shifted and the vision broadened beyond the hierarchical. But tensions multiplied too. Role definitions, gifts, responsibilities and relationships became new points of theological departure. People, in other words, who do not "belong" to a Church but are the Church begin to take that focus seriously and in ways that alter past patterns and beliefs.

Divine Revelation

In this document a new emphasis on the place of Scripture in Catholic formation re-energized the disciplines of literary exegesis and historical scholarship—disciplines which had been dormant in Roman circles for years. This was a real turning point in catechetical orientation. Cooperation with Protestant scholars, too, would go a long way to bridge the Catholic-Protestant gulf. At the same time, this fresh encouragement of biblical study raised new issues as well. The relationship of developing scholarship to defined interpretation or tradition is a central question, but the question of whether revelation is on-going may be even more problematic as tradition is contested in favor of new insights with scriptural foundation.

The Constitution on the Liturgy

The turning point of this document lay in its pristine approach to Eucharistic celebration. The institution of the vernacular as an "official" language of consecration, the concern for participation and the endorsement of cultural adaptation were all geared to return the liturgy to the people—the Church. Gone was the notion that Eucharist was a single priest in a darkened crypt whose goal was to "get something in." It was all a breakthrough for Christian community.

But tensions lurked in these shadows too. Uniformity—the long-heralded counterpoint of catholicity—became a point of contention which led to concerns about authority and "unity, essence and catholicity." The liturgy became a battleground where bread recipes, ministers and translations were centers of conflict and control. Things once considered essential became questionable; mystique became confused with mystery.

The Church in the Modern World

In this statement the Council redefined the relationship between the Roman Catholic Church and the world around it. From an insular perspective which emphasized the separateness of the sacred and secular domains, the Church in Vatican II turned squarely to the consideration of the integrity of the two. From a posture of resistance and rejection, the Church turned to a commitment to human advancement, the development of world community, the acceptance of science and a new concern for the economic and cultural development of all peoples as well as their spiritual salvation. The transformation of society is thus publicly declared in this key document as an essential part of the Church's mission to humanity.

And so the tensions are clear: though the Church in this new age has declared a truce with science, someone must still ask when what is technically possible is morally appropriate. Or worse, how can the Church be a corporate witness without being simply socially manipulative? Or, more directly, how much involvement is too much involvement of the Church in the political system and political issues? When does advocacy become control? And when we argue for moral principles in the marketplace, whose morality shall it be and who decides?

The answers are slow in coming.

Communication

The statement on Church and communications is clearer for its effect fifteen years after its development than it was at the time of its implications. Television evangelism was only at its beginnings when the Council adopted this positive approach to modern media. With it, old questions of control and censorship and conflict abated a bit. But the new questions of packaging, of the rise of an electronic Church with its consequences of remoteness, slickness and commercial competition were laid bare and will probably cause tension for a while to come.

Ecumenism/Relationship with Eastern Catholicism

Though they are certainly not concerned with exactly the same questions, we can consider them together in terms of the openness that is the turning point in each of them. These two documents recognize officially the scandal of Christian division. What is more, the statement asserts a unity in vision and essential commitment while affirming the diversity of gifts—liturgical, spiritual and theological— which make up the Church of Christ in all its denominations. New tensions derive from precisely these admissions. They bring the Church beyond past tensions to a public recognition of a common Christian charism, so the challenge of moving ecumenism beyond ecclesiastical get-togethers to the recognition of the single mission of the total Christian Church means that this role in mission can and must be shared, that indifferentism is not ecumenism and that, on the other hand, absolutism erodes the witness of the full Christian presence. Conversion and repentance, in other words, are imperatives of the Church as well as of its members.

The Decree on the Bishops' Pastoral Office in the Church

The turn from medieval hierarchy to modern pastor is the central point of this text. The bishop, consequently, is not defined as lord and lawgiver. His role rather is to enable the Church, to be in touch with issues and ideas, to create a national identity. The question of international control of the newly heightened local church is never mentioned but surely that tension derives in large part from this new orientation.

On Priesthood and Priestly Formation

These two documents may someday be seen as pivotal to the development of the new Church which the earlier documents point to. Here clericalism dies. The priest is asked to be able to form community, to lead the search for God but to acknowledge, listen to and trust the laity whose gifts are essential to the Church. As a "brother among brothers" the priest is to be a spiritual catalyst, not a parish potentate. But the role revision sounds a great deal easier to effect in theory than it is in practice. The tensions, in fact, derive from the very theological shift that should minimize them.

In the first place the question of pastoral leadership depends, at least in part, upon the ability of the priest to understand, communicate and affirm the equal gifts of others—e.g., the married and women—and to build communities of ministering Christians. It depends as well then on the acceptance and respect of that community. From a position of "father," the priest is asked to assume the role of "brother," a not insignificant transition which will be taxing for everyone concerned.

On Religious Life

Over four hundred years after the Council of Trent cast religious life in stone, Vatican Council II called it to renewal. More importantly, perhaps, the Council instructed religious to turn to the Gospels, the initiating intent of their founders and the social realities of the times—not to Church law or episcopal control—for their criteria and direction. They were, moreover, to direct the chief facets of their lives—life-style, work and prayer—to changes based on the physical and psychological needs of their members and the social and economic needs of the culture in which they ministered.

The tensions surfaced almost immediately and are manifest still. The dualistic notion that the essence of religious perfection lies in separation from the world lingers still. Transcending the world, then, becomes a counterweight to transforming it. Consequently, renewal becomes a struggle to balance the claims of law against the touchstone of experience. Finally the question of whether religious life is to be fundamentally charismatic or functionally institutional remains a determining issue. It will be years, it seems, before it is clear how many streams will be turned by the river of religious renewal. It may take even longer to assess which river will run strongest.

Decree on the Laity

That the role of the laity in the Church was even an issue at Vatican II may be the greatest turning point of the Church's modern history. For, in this decree, the lay state in the Church began to be described as a vocation. Multiple charisms were reaffirmed and lay members were instructed that the believer "has both a right and a duty to use them." Participation rather than passivity became a factor of commitment. From that rationale came the call to responsibility for Church organization, for Catholic education and formation programs, for Church administration itself.

The inherent tension in this development of the laity is at least twofold. First, this departure from clericalism in the Catholic community raises the issue of ascribed and achieved authority. When the competence lies with the lay leader, to what degree is the priest in charge of parish direction or the school, for instance? In the second place, if the laity are really gifted for the sake of the Christian community, does this mean lay women too, or only lay men? And if it does mean women, why are they not being accepted in worship or administration? If I were a Roman Catholic bishop in this country, I would not be disturbed that Catholic women want to minister in the Church. I would be worried that they must go to Protestant seminaries for the theological and pastoral preparation to do it. If Roman

Catholic schools and dioceses continue to refuse to prepare women for participation in the Church, I predict that this movement of Catholic women to Protestant schools of theology will significantly alter the shape of the Church in twenty-five years.

Decree on Missionary Activity

The turning point in this Vatican II document is attitudinally so deep that perhaps only a Catholic can sense its real depth. Two new postures are affirmed here. First, conversion must be free—the faith does not follow the flag. With this statement hundreds of years of Church-state control are abandoned in favor of Church-state separation. For a Church whose entire middle history was embedded in theistic governments, the philosophical departure, though late, is not to go unnoticed. For with this new official stance comes the second notion. Missionaries are to be presence more than proselyte. They are to inculturate the Church among the people and, as quickly as possible, to make the Church native in clergy, education and custom. According to the document, at least, Western ecclesiastical imperialism is over.

However, this growing shift in the center of the Church from first to third world peoples in population, character and tone has done little or nothing to dislodge Roman curial control. Tension is inherent here. How long new native churches will tolerate Western formulations, interpretations and theology is anybody's guess.

Decree on Christian Education

An especially interesting facet of these Vatican documents is that an entire statement is dedicated to Christian education. There is, after all, no similar statement on Christian social service or justice programs. Nevertheless, even this statement is built on a turning point. For the first time, the educational mission of the Church is related to participation in social, economic and political realities as well as simply to catechetical purposes.

What this specific attention may signal, however, is the concentration of Church resources on a single aspect of society to such an extent that the ability to function elsewhere is actually impaired. Unless this balance is maintained the Church could find itself someday without presence in other vital areas of human life and also without an effective school system. Once priced out of the educational market, its mission would be not to the ignorant and disenfranchised but to the rich and powerful.

The Relationship of the Church to Non-Christian Religions

The turning point of this document is simply the realization that a time bomb is waiting to go off. In a dramatic move, this declaration from a council of the Church solemnly assembled asserts that as Christians we must accept "all that is true and holy" in Buddhism, Hinduism, Islam and Judaism. After centuries of repudiation, moreover, the Church officially condemns in this statement any persecution or discrimination based on race, color, condition of life or religion. The implications for world development and the creation of human community are far-ranging but late and incomplete.

No consciousness of sexism emerges in this document. No preparation for its position exists in the Roman Catholic community. The residual tensions in both those realities are yet to be recognized but, I submit, very real.

The Decree on Religious Freedom

The revolutionary tenet of this document is simply that conscience must be the primary determinant of religious conviction. Everyone then is immune from coercion in the name of religion. The problem is clear: Someone, somewhere must come to grips with coercion. Is legislative pressure to write morality into law "coercion"? And, if it is not, whose morality shall it be? How much political involvement is Christian? What is the line between Church and state?

What the Council fathers addressed looked clear, almost medieval in some aspects, when it was written. In the light of present political conditions, it is ablaze and new.

The analysis is brief and broad-brushed but highlights at least several threads that bear further focus:

1. The papers are compatible in orientation and theology but apparently unmindful of the realities which counterpoint the turns they set in motion.

2. This new ideology, though laudable, is constrained in its development by the old structures and old laws which obstruct or smother it.

3. Important life questions are raised in these documents which nevertheless remain even untreated, let alone resolved. The issues of celibacy, women, priesthood, laity and centralization are embedded in these renewal decrees and will press for resolution for years to come.

The cultural drag between conceptualization and internalization is no more evident than in the aftermath of a revolutionary Ecumenical Council. Inversely, the rate of change—both slow and fast—that follows is itself alienating. What is just as bad is the confusion of the simple whose religion has been reduced to pious absolutes. At the same time there is no substitute for the vision, the integrity, the hope that is generated when a Church measures itself by the depth of the Gospel.

It is this Christian tradition that echoes best the full history of the Church. For at another time, in another place, the Church had dealt with the tension between insight and implementation and that polarization has marked the Church of unity ever since. In Acts 11, Peter is given a vision of the possible: What God has purified, you are not to call unclean. In Galatians 2, after Peter has succumbed to social pressure and the security of past traditions, withdrawing in the face of criticism and difficulty, Paul calls him to it.

The point is that once again in the Church's quest for renewal, its central issue is the need to summon the conscience of Peter, the courage of Paul.

10. A FITTING SYMBOL

The ordination of women to the priesthood has not been the central issue in my personal life. I have never been against it—in fact, I found the very discussion of the question a fascinating indicator of the type of world to come and looked forward to it. On the other hand, I myself have been concentrating more on what I thought were the pressing and the immediate woman issues: the right to equal educational opportunities, economic equality, civil rights, equality of status and position or, in the case of women religious, community self-determination. The recent Vatican Declaration, "Women in the Ministerial Priesthood," however, raises such questions in my mind about the effect of "maleness" on the integrity of the faith itself.

The proper symbol of Christ, says the recent Declaration, is male. If that is so, then many other things are not: that Christ is God, that both women and men are bound to be "other Christs," that sacraments are effective by virtue of the power of God, that grace makes new creations of us all.

The Vatican Congregation for the Doctrine of the Faith, through this publication, has brought the Church to a moment of crucial reflection. For the first time since the Council of Trent, a Vatican document has purported by offical statement to declare the inadmissibility of women to priesthood and to "clarify this by the analogy of faith" or consistency of its teaching. The explanation itself, however, is based on arguments that themselves introduce inconsistency into the Christian tradition.

Prior to this time, and even now in some parts of the world or in some people in our own, the female priest is socially unacceptable. The male-dominated society which fostered this exclusion is a direct outgrowth of notions of male and female that were based on faulty understandings of biology, on social systems that depended for their existence on physical force, on false psychologies that promoted the education of men but not of women, on primitive blood taboos, on the incorrect identification of the man as life-giver.

Not only were women not priests in societies such as these, they were also not doctors or teachers or actors or mayors or senators either. Some of these understandings remain as residual influences in this society and account for the slow, difficult pace of woman's movement to full and equal humanity.

The Vatican Declaration against the ordination of women priests does not use these arguments, but one is tempted to wonder whether or not these are not yet really the underlying assumptions, since the verbalized explanation so directly contradicts basic Catholic teaching. The point the document makes is that a priest must be male so that the historical Christ can be "fittingly" imaged, represented or symbolized.

In the words of the document itself, the explanation reads:

". . . the bishop or priest, in the exercise of his ministry, does not act in his own name, *in persona propria:* he represents Christ, who acts through him. . . .

". . . this representation is found in the altogether special form in the celebration of the Eucharist (in which) the priest . . . acts not only through the effective power conferred on him by Christ, but *in persona Christi,* taking the role of Christ, to the point of being his very image.

". . . the priest is a sign . . . that must be perceptible and that the faithful must be able to recognize with ease.

". . . the whole sacramental economy is in fact based on natural signs, on symbols imprinted on the human psychology."

This use of symbolism as an explanation for the male priesthood raises in me several serious questions:

1. What is a symbol, a sign, an image, a representative?

2. What is being symbolized in the priesthood and its supreme moment, the Mass?

3. What is being communicated by this kind of sign?

The document uses the terms "symbol," "sign," "representative" and "image" as the central concepts supporting an exclusively male priesthood. The problem lies in the fact that the interchangeable use of these terms calls into question the traditional explanations of what is being symbolized "in the altogether special form of the Eucharist."

Briefly, *symbols* are generally defined as "visible signs of something invisible" and are therefore charged with meaning; *signs,* on the other hand, indicate or refer to particular information or specific things, events or conditions which stand in literal or one-to-one correlation; *representatives* portray or act as agents for another; *images* give likeness.

If nothing invisible is being commemorated in the Mass, then a sign or representative of the man Jesus is sufficient. If, however, as Church doctrine maintains, the Mass is the re-creation of God's saving plan for humanity, then more needs to be communicated than the simple act of the Last Supper event for which only a male figure will really do. But we have been led to believe more.

The question becomes then whether or not it is the purpose and total meaning of the Mass simply to recall the historical Jesus and, if so, is even the male priest an adequate sign of that?

Other teachings tell us that Jesus was both God and man and had the properties of both. If indeed this is the case there are interesting implications of this reality that must be brought to bear on any discussion of who is or is not a proper candidate for orders. God we believe from earliest tradition, both Judaic and Christian, is neither male nor female but, in the fullness of ineffable mystery and nature, both. God says, in Genesis: "Let us make man in our image, in the likeness of ourselves" and "in the image of God, male and female he created them." In this passage, too, God is called *Elohim,* a feminine noun with a masculine plural ending. The point is that the "image" of God includes both male and female. In that case, it can be inferred that Christ, who is God as well as man, is also inadequately imaged by one sex alone and only. In fact, among the many traditional symbols of Christ, two—the pelican who feeds her young and the mermaid whose dual nature signified the humanity and divinity of Jesus—are clearly female renderings which emphasize the androgynous nature of Christ.

Furthermore, though it is true that the incarnation assumes the male sex it is also true that the male but not the female sex was bypassed in the very process. The point is that though males are certainly closer types or pictures of Christ's humanity they are no more a symbol of his divinity than women who in their person also recall the humanity of his birth.

God's self-identity "I am who am" led the Israelites to forbid the creation of images that purported to identify and therefore limit the nature of God. The immanent tragedy is that the Church, despite social evolution and the developments of theology and science, stands on the brink of perpetuating an image of maleness in God's very name. The intent and disposition of the minister, we have always been told, are not necessary to the sacramental act, but apparently maleness is. In the spiritual order of things, that is a difficult conclusion to draw.

What the present Declaration seems to intend with its argument for an exclusively male priesthood, then, is an historical description rather than the communication of the essential elements of sacrifice, re-creation, reconciliation and redemption.

As the Declaration itself maintains, signs and symbols must be "easily perceptible." What is not made conscious in the document is the fact that something becomes symbolic to a group because it conjures up for them common associations or meanings outside itself which speak to the group itself, its relationships or its fundamental purposes.

Consequently, as the group's understanding of itself changes, its symbols must also change. When American settlers saw themselves as British citizens, the Union Jack and the Crown were important symbols of their identity. Once they saw themselves as a people distinct in place and purpose, they communicated themselves differently: as a collection of separate stars, an independent eagle.

As the followers of Jesus saw themselves less a Jewish sect and more a universal Church, their symbols changed, too.

Now, more and more, the Christian community becomes aware that the subordination of women—a result of the fall—is also lifted by Christ's death and resurrection. "To put on Christ" is the right and responsibility of all of us, male and female. And if not the right, then it is not the responsibility either.

To maintain a symbol-system that is actually incomplete in its theological consciousness is to leave the Church with nothing but an historical sign of its very being. The questions the document raises for me need more of an answer than that to satisfy the fullness of a creation whose likeness is "made in the image of God, male and female he created them."

11. THE SIN OF SILENCE—
THE SOUNDS OF CARE

The agitation burned in me like fire. I was agitated with myself.

The sign on the front of the display booth in the Pittsburgh airport read: "Build More Nukes. Feed Jane Fonda to the Whales." When I confronted the young man behind the counter in the neat business suit about the callousness of the presentation he explained, patronizingly, "We're only trying to get the liberals to develop a little sense of humor, ma'am."

Later that same month, the Physicians for the Prevention of Nuclear War, Inc., an international organization of prominent doctors, met to begin a campaign intended to build resistance to the design and use of nuclear weapons in the militaries of the world. They said:

> How can we dispel the notion of some people that anyone will survive a nuclear war? How can we as doctors influence people to prevent any further buildup of nuclear arms? The medical profession should more actively protest against the senseless policy of increasing arsenals of thermonuclear arms.

Then, a week after that, President Jimmy Carter in his last address to the nation before leaving office warned:

> The [nuclear] danger is becoming greater. As the arsenals of the superpowers grow in size and sophistication and as other governments—perhaps even, in the future, dozens of governments—acquire these weapons, it may only be a matter of time before

102

madness, desperation, greed or miscalculation lets loose this terrible force. . . . The United States and all countries must find ways to control and to reduce the horrifying danger that is posed by the enormous world stockpiles of nuclear arms.

All of these positions agitated me—not because I lack humor, not simply because a president made what could conceivably have been a purely political statement, not because I'm afraid to die in a nuclear war. On the contrary, I am much more apprehensive about surviving one.

No, the positions affected me because they brought to the surface for one more agonizing time the reality of insanity—mine as well as the nation's. I realized then that I'd been writing this chapter for months—perhaps for years—and the process had been painful, barren, threatening. It's so delicate a subject—not the business-as-usual material on ministry or leadership or the standard theology of religious life. This chapter had something to do with me, with my life, with what my very existence is about.

The commitment it reflects has not come easily. It has not, in fact, completely clarified yet. But it is embedded in who I am as a Benedictine, as a woman and as an educator. On these points, at least, I'm ready now.

As an educator, I am first of all, confused and concerned by the language that masks the reality of the nuclear age. To distance ourselves from the unacceptable effects of nuclear annihilation, we use words with acceptable overtones or connotations. We talk about surgical strike or precisely targeted attacks, presumably on military installations, as if in a nuclear attack there could really be contained contamination. Americans, of course, feel strongly that anything "surgical" is curative, humanitarian, of lofty purpose. What could possibly be wrong with anything so controlled, so pure of heart, unless, of course, what is to be excised is a tumor in the brain: Norad in Colorado City, for instance, the Pentagon in Washington, D.C., or Rocky Flats in Denver—all obvious sites of attack in case of nuclear war and all in heavily populated and vital areas, all said now to be able to be removed "surgically"?

We fail, in other words, to recognize that even in a so-called surgical strike the "cure" may be as deadly as the disease. The operation may indeed succeed but the patient will be permanently disabled nevertheless.

"Attack" would be so much more honest a word. The purpose would be clearer; the effects more understandable. Why don't we simply say "attack" and "destroy" and "annihilate" and "contaminate" because that is what we are really prepared to do?

When I discovered that "collateral damage" was military terminology for the civilian deaths to be expected in nuclear conflict, I realized how far away we've strayed from our consciousness or care of human life no matter what our national self-image might be. People had become "units of loss" rather than names or personalities or family figures. People had become tallies on our war-game charts whose destruction we figure with pride.

I began to cringe at the comedic acronyms—SAINT, HALO, BAMBI—we were using to make the sinister, the satanic perhaps, benign characters in the national fairy tale. Only one, MAD—Mutually Assured Destruction—a term used to describe our ability to retaliate with equally incapacitating force—signaled the psychotic state of the nation and my own contribution to it.

I began to resent the scientific jargon that made the military Scrabble game a tower of nationalist Babel. The widow next door, the high school senior, the welder of car fenders, the hard-hat bricklayer know about security and freedom and the Halls of Montezuma and Gettysburg. On the other hand they may not really understand that behind the high-sounding technological gobbledygook—ICBM, B-1 bomber, MX missile system, megatons—lie hair-trigger weaponry that is capable of wiping out entire cities of people as simple as themselves, but they are certainly awed and impressed into accepting silence by the cold complexity of titles.

I began to suspect the talk about nuclear "defense" which acknowledged all the while that the only way to defend oneself from nuclear destruction was to strike first—which means that someone will have to judge when that has become necessary, and which means that we are prepared to strike first and be wrong rather than to trust. But I began to see, too, that the country that strikes first will have nothing to claim, that the entire world economy could collapse as a result, that first-strike nations will strike themselves at the same time.

The madness began to be too, too plain to me; my too common common sense began to wither.

And then I realized that the people are not meant to understand. Because, though simple people want to defend their own security and lives, they really do not—most of them—really want to take anyone else's—not massively, not indiscriminately, not savagely. And the language solves that. What can be savage that is so scientific? Long ago the do-able became the desirable in the Western world; long ago technology became God and the schizophrenic language of science its liturgy.

As an educator I began to know that it is not that we are so close to a nuclear mind-set that had begun to bother me. It is that despite its ominous and general presence we are so far away from it: twenty-year-olds sit at the bottom of missile silos with their fingers over launch buttons while a world that can already destroy itself once stockpiles to do it one hundred times. They will never see the faces of their victims, never watch civilian babies die, never see the world's farmlands shrivel. They will never have to see the consequences of their actions. They will simply know that they have been "surgical," "innocent," "scientific."

I have found myself, in other words, in the long struggle to understand the nuclear issue, hardened by its language, diminished by its distance, lied to. As an educator I had come to a dead end. "Thy speech hath betrayed thee" rang in my ears.

But there were even deeper dimensions to my developing consciousness. I was a Benedictine and a woman. I had to ask myself in the face of these realities what it now meant to be both.

To be Benedictine was the most burdensome blessing of all. The monastic life had long been defined as ascetic, other-wordly, withdrawn. Good monks and nuns—the nineteenth-century understanding went—were to struggle to transcend an evil world, to remove themselves from its secular concerns, to be above the interests or problems of their times. Gone for ages was the memory of the monastery as the center of the city, of the monastic as leader and leaven.

To be Benedictine and monastic no longer meant to see what others were not sensitive to, to do what others had not done, to cry Gospel in a guarded world. The monastic life had become pious, passive and protected. Separation of Church and state had brought us to the point where it was now considered sacrilegious for the Christian to call the conscience of the king.

We were a long way from the social and pacifist tradition that was basic to the Benedictine life and the Church from which it sprang.

But I knew that it was monastic communities which in earlier times had taken personal responsibility for the shaping of human community. This Benedictine posture was evident through centuries of disease, poverty and public calamity. Intervening to assert the right of all to share in the wealth of God's creation, monasteries organized relief before state agencies existed. During the time of usurious lending, Benedictines established a system of monastic mortgages with loans at reasonable rates and gave interest-free loans to aid victims of natural catastrophe. Hospitality extended to nobles, prisoners, indigents, social outcasts and slaves.

And I remembered that in his *Life of Antony,* Athanasius had written of that monk's confrontation with the civil system:

> When the judge saw the fearlessness of Antony and of those with him, he issued the order that none of the monks were to appear in the law court, nor were they to stay in the city at all. All the others thought it was wise to go into hiding that day, but Antony took this so seriously as to wash his upper garment and to stand the next day in a prominent place in front and to be clearly visible to the prefect. When, while all marveled at this, the prefect, passing by with his escort, saw him, he stood there calmly, demonstrating the purposefulness that belongs to us Christians.

I was moved to admit that there had been no room in my own religious formation for these kinds of witness.

I realized, too, that from the earliest centuries, both monks and clerics had claimed exemption from military service on the grounds that those who were intent on modeling the Christ-life simply could not kill. I became keenly aware that it was Benedictines whose most ancient motto was Pax, that it was Benedictines who had provided sanctuary during the medieval wars, that it was the Benedictine Order that was credited with having once saved Western civilization. I became convinced that the kind of leadership brought by Benedictines to the framing of the Truce of God and the Peace of God during the wars of the Middle Ages was needed again in our own time.

To be monastic, I began to think, was to have burning eyes and a prophet's steel voice. As Benedictine I was compelled to face the nuclear issue. But if to be Benedictine in the nuclear age was decisive in my commitment to nuclear disarmament, to be a woman was determinative.

In the nuclear arms race, I saw all the male values of the society run amok. Competition, profit and power have all conspired to bring the world to the edge of its own destruction. Like bullies on the block, the world has gathered its gangs to fight to the death to protect what they don't have a right to in the first place.

Who is best and who is right and who is richest have become the control questions of the human race. Universal political, economic and social issues are being deterred in their resolution by military threat. Macho. Pure macho.

It is nurturance and imagination that are needed, openness and compassion that are missing; trust and vulnerability that we lack. It is the feminine view of the world that has too long been disregarded.

As a woman whose life has been too often predicated on patriarchal norms, I realized that I had had enough of all that. Because the economy depends on the military industry, because the Army wants destructive power to rival the Navy's, because we want to be on top—these are not reasons I now find compelling. Lesser values are not good enough anymore.

G. K. Chesterton once wrote: "It is not that Christianity has been tried and found wanting. Christianity has not been tried."

We are surely at the point where we must all try again—together.

It is out of these perspectives that all the arguments for the arms race fall away. If the Russians were really coming, they could—by our own calculations—easily have come by now. If deterrence is the issue, we can, by our own calculations, already destroy the world one hundred times. Isn't once enough?

In the face of irreparable damage or the total destruction of this world, I remember another holocaust and Elie Wiesel's indictment: "And the world was silent." I remember that people were silent as ten thousand people a day were methodically destroyed: six million

107

Jews, one million Jewish children—in the name of someone's national ideals.

Now they say, "No one will ever use nuclear weapons; that's exactly why we build them." But we did. *We* did.

I remember too that now we can eliminate, contaminate, erase, a culture just as easily as the Nazis exterminated the Jews. I know, in fact, that we plan to do so if and when we decide it's necessary. I know we call it "surgical strike"—methodical, calculated, idealistic.

I was there when Elie Wiesel threw back in our religious faces the final challenge: "If the victim is my problem then the killer is yours. I must ask why Jews walked silently, docilely to their deaths. You must ask how a Christian could murder Jews—one million Jewish children—and remain a Christian. You must ask why no Pope ever excommunicated them."

Elie Wiesel, Jewish writer and survivor of the German death camps at Auschwitz and Birchenau, is intent on reminding people what it is to exterminate a nation. He is keeping the memory of the horror alive in this generation so that another age does not repeat the barbarism. Elie Wiesel is trying to make us confront this era's sin of silence.

As an educator, as a Benedictine, as a woman I fear this generation's sin of silence.

12. WOMEN RELIGIOUS WITNESS FOR PEACE

There is a story told among Hasidic Jews that I think is important for Christians, important for Pentecost. This story is about a wise old rabbi whose insights were so clear, whose teachings so profound, that not only his own congregation but the rabbis in congregations of villages beyond the mountains looked to him for leadership. Then suddenly he died.

The young rabbis prayed sincerely for the infusion of that same kind of spirit, and, sure enough, one night the old master appeared to one of them in sleep.

The young man said, "Master, it's good that you've returned. Our people look to us for answers to the great questions of life and we do not know them all. Tell us, Master: On the other side, of what account are the sins of youth?"

And the old man said, "The sins of youth? Why, on the other side the sins of youth are of no account whatsoever."

And the young rabbi said, "The sins of youth are of no account whatsoever? Then what has it all been about? What is punishable on the other side?"

And the old man said, "That sin which is punishable on the other side with continual and unending severity is the sin of false piety."

I submit with the Hasidim that true fear of God demands that we know what piety is proper for our times.

It is easy to pray for the gifts of the Holy Spirit if it's the love of praying that prompts us and not the gifts themselves. But if we've come here today because we're intent on Pentecost and not simply on praying, then I beg all of you, beware—because the gifts of the

Holy Spirit are not gifts for getting and keeping; the gifts of the Holy Spirit are gifts for giving and doing.

The gifts of the Holy Spirit are not meant to simply condition and console. Of course wisdom, understanding, fortitude and counsel are important; the revelation, the insights, the endurance and the direction they bring are surely and certainly necessary, even imperative. But our own consolation is not what Pentecost is all about. The flaming gifts of the Holy Spirit do not simply console. They commit; they compel; they cost; they cry out for creative change.

"Rabbi," the disciples demanded, "we pray; we fast; we read the Scriptures. Why has the Messiah not come?" And the rabbi replied: "Wherefore did the son of Jesse not come, neither yesterday nor today? The Messiah does not come today because today we are no different than we were yesterday."

From this moment on, for us that can never be true again. Tomorrow you and I will be different. Perhaps we will not be better, but we must definitely be different, because we have come today to pray the presence of Pentecost into our own lives. We have come together at this moment for gifts of piety, for knowledge, for fear of our God.

But do not be misled. We have not come here to pray for pietism; we have come to pray *for piety.* We have not come here to pray for the grace to practice private devotion; we have come to pray for dedication to the public, dutiful service of God.

To pray for piety is to pray for the gifts of leadership and courage, strength and risk, gifts of which the Book of Wisdom speaks when it praises "those pious ones, your ancestors" who have gone before us: Moses and Aaron; Joshua and Caleb; Samuel and Solomon—leaders, judges, prophets, risk-takers all. We have come to pray for the piety to which Jesus called the Pharisees over and over again.

There are those who say that on Pentecost religious should be in their convents, not in Washington, D.C. There are those who say that religious should mind their prayers, not the morality of politics. There are those who say that religious should concentrate on acts of mercy and forget the obstacles to justice. So domesticated has our piety become that it has become unreligious for religious to call the conscience of the king. Tell that to Jeremiah and Daniel, to Deborah and Judith.

We have to come to pray for knowledge—not for technical specialization but for a burning vision of the integrity between the sacred and the secular, the present and the eternal. And we have never needed knowledge more. In 1945 with the detonation of the atomic bomb, we witnessed one of the great watersheds of history when a whole new age began. It was as distinct from the age that preceded it as the modern age was distinct from the Middle Ages, as the Middle Ages were distinct from antiquity.

Thirty-seven Pentecosts ago the old rules of war became obsolete; the old theologies of war became amusing; the old methods of war became meaningless because what nuclear weapons seek to preserve, they can only destroy. What we value we must preserve some other way or not preserve it at all. Until then we will have "defenses" that undermine domestic development and are incapable of promoting peace.

They take from the poor: We have reduced social welfare funding by $57 billion in two years.

They terrorize the vulnerable: We have increased our military spending by $33 billion in one year.

They are based on national suicide and national insolvency, not on national security.

They have replaced the welfare state with the military state. We have diverted our national wealth and resources away from housing, away from poverty, away from research, away from the arts.

We have chosen to be Sparta, rather than Athens.

Viktor Frankl, the Jewish psychiatrist and survivor of German concentration camps, says that in time of crisis people do one of three things: They deny it. ("It's not that bad. It will never happen.") They despair. ("There is nothing anyone can do. We must simply live through it and pray.") Or they commit themselves to ask critical questions. Perhaps you and I, being who we are, cannot really do much, but we can at least give the gift of Christian discomfort. By knowing enough to say no, we can make it impossible for anyone to make war easily. And we can give others the knowledge it takes to do the same.

111

We are praying, too, for a holy fear of God. We have learned to fear the Unknown Other, but have forgotten to fear the just God who made them as well as us.

We have learned to fear trust, but have forgotten to fear the insidious effects of Christian schizophrenia. We talk peace but we prepare for annihilation.

We have learned to fear the enemy but we have forgotten to fear ourselves, though it is we who invented the first atomic bomb, we who produced the first hydrogen bomb, we who deployed the first armed ICBMs, we who invented multiple warheads.

We have not feared to wage the weapons of war, but we have feared to wage peace with the same intensity.

In 1980 the annual budget for the Commission on Arms Control and Disarmament was less than half what the Department of Defense spends on military bands. To those who say "Isn't deterrence essential?" I say: "Isn't once enough?"

Yes, we will be different tomorrow if we pray seriously for piety, for knowledge, for fear of our God, but we will not necessarily be better. For though the gifts of the Holy Spirit can be enspiriting, they can be sinned against too. The sin against piety is to choose private devotion rather than our public duties to creation. The sin against knowledge is to know that something must be done but then do nothing at all. The sin against the fear of God is to be silent in a world that is both materially and morally underdeveloped.

The possible power of Pentecost, in other words, is the power not to give over our own power to people who want to name our enemies. No, we must stand instead like Esther, who went to the king though she was not called; like Judith, who put herself between the besieging army and her defenseless people because any other defense would have been totally destructive.

We must not stand like Samson, who teaches us the tragic and fatal combination of power and blindness without the union of strength and vision. Yes, Samson brought the temple down upon his enemies, but Samson destroyed himself as well. That is the message of Pentecost to our times. Certainly our strength cannot be impaired in this country, but our vision can be lost. We can and we must realize from Samson that there is nothing more dangerous than a frustrated, frightened giant who fears the wrong things.

Remember too that if you have asked for the gifts today, the gifts are ours to give—to speak the truth in public, to say no and to teach others to say no, to distinguish piety from patriotism, to distinguish knowledge from nationalism, to distinguish the fear of force from fear of God, to renew our own lives, to renew a universal concern for others, to renew the face of the earth.

What can we do? We can learn in our time from the pieties of the past. An ancient monastic tale recounts that a religious who wanted to be holy said to the spiritual guide: "According as I am able, I keep my little rule; I do my little fast, my prayer, my meditation, my contemplative silence, and according as I am able I strive to cleanse my heart from evil thoughts. Now, holy one, what more should I do?"

The elder rose up, stretched her hands all the way to heaven, and her fingers became like ten lamps of fire. And the holy one said, "If you want to be holy, why not be totally changed into fire?"

What more can we do? We keep our little fasts, sign our little cards, wear our little buttons, say our prayers and cleanse our hearts of evil thoughts. But more than that, we too can arm. We can arm ourselves with piety, with knowledge, with the fear of our God.

Whether we are received at those White House gates or not, we can, as holy people of our time, exert a powerful feminine influence in a world reeling from macho-mania. We can, if we want, if we truly want, if we deeply want at this new Pentecost point, be turned, you and I, courageously, consumingly, completely, into new Pentecost fire.

In every convent, in every church, in every state, for God's sake, why are we not being turned totally into fire?

13. THE ROLE OF RELIGIOUS COMMUNITIES IN THE PEACE MOVEMENT: TO TEACH HOLY DISOBEDIENCE

In the environment that spawned World War II, Gertrude Stein said that the most important thing for Germans to learn was disobedience. In 1973 an American sociologist, Gerda Lederer, did a large-scale comparative study of authoritarianism in West German and American adolescents. Authoritarianism—the willingness to submit to authority and the need to dominate others—had been a pre-war hallmark of Nazi Germany. Prepared by Bismarck's military regime and nourished by Hitler through the Nazi Youth Corps, this disposition to blind obedience to official command was later pointed to by social psychologists to explain the compliance of German Christians in the Jewish holocaust. The astonishing conclusion of Lederer's study was that by 1973 German teenagers had become even less authoritarian than their American counterparts even though they had much further to come in their development of anti-authoritarian principles.

What may be even more telling are the findings of Stanley Milgram from 1966–1974. Nearly two-thirds of the participants in a study to determine the degree to which subjects were willing to inflict pain on another individual simply because they had been directed to do so by an authority figure complied completely. They never questioned either the reasons or the results of their actions. They simply followed orders on the assumption that if they had been told by an official that their cooperation in this violence was necessary, then indeed it must be. To make matters worse, D. C. Bock researched the relationship between religious beliefs and obedience to destructive commands and concluded: "Religious beliefs and behaviors are related to obedience. A clear trend of refusal to yield to authority was noted in non-believers. Moderate believers were consistently high in the delivery of shock, but believers were the most obedient, delivering more shock than any other group."

The tragedy is that religious communities themselves have been so instrumental in living and teaching this brand of obedience.

Every day people that the churches have educated go quietly and serenely to factories where they assemble warheads, to laboratories where they increase the megaton capacity of our arsenals, to boardrooms where they vote to increase our "defense" capabilities, to churches where they pray the Our Father without discomfort.

The role of the religious community in such a culture is surely a clear one. It is of course to pray for peace, not to cajole God to save us from our own insane sinfulness but to make ourselves receptive to God's in-breaking in our lives and culture. It is as well to be centers of peace where strangers can become sisters or brothers in Christ. It is, finally, to become models of disobedience. Fromm describes the "revolutionary personality" as a person who is independent, who has the capacity to identify deeply with humanity and who has the ability to disobey in the interest of more fundamental values. The prophets, Christ, the early Christians would understand the role completely. It is up to the religious of this day, who take a public vow of obedience to God, to reclaim and recall a conforming world to the burning burden of that promise.

14. THE LEADERSHIP NEEDED IN RELIGIOUS LIFE

This year's assembly, Sisters, presents a terrible temptation for someone who is first on a program. The temptation is to drift into metaphor and to be poetic. The call, if this is a call, is not intended to be that. It is intended to be what is, from my point of view, an honest analysis of the present alternatives in religious life. The assembly which we are opening tonight is a public admission of unfinishedness called "journey." It is also therefore a public proclamation of a continuing commitment to grow. The Benedictines call it "to seek God," who ever calls anew.

In 1968 we, the women in this room, most of us, began to call ourselves to rigorous self-assessment. That year was a beginning. Tonight, in utter seriousness, we call ourselves not only to consider where we are—we have done so much of that—but to begin to proclaim together and publicly where women religious, after ten years of searching, are beginning to feel that religious life must go. The presentation I make tonight is meant to be a backdrop to that effort.

Before we begin the week, then, I submit for your consideration three items: what I consider to be a model of religious life, a description of its current situation, and an analysis of the challenges which I personally believe confront those of us who are in leadership positions in religious communities today.

The model is a motley one. It is from 2 Kings 6—7. It is a very simple but graphic story and you probably remember it well. Samaria, the writer says, is suffering siege and the situation is very extreme. The city has been surrounded for so long that within the walls they lack, for the first time in their conscious history, both water and food, the very staples of life. The bony heads of asses are being sold for eighty shekels and are the supper of nobles. The women of the poor have even begun to plot how to identify which of their children will be eaten first. And, outside, the enemy makes no move to attack.

There is no reason to attack. They can simply wait for the Israelites within the city to die, because Israel has lost its inner resources, its energy and its will to confront its real problems. Instead they go on, day after day, business as usual, and wait for Yahweh to save them. These Israelites in this city apparently don't notice, or at least they certainly don't care, about four lepers who in this period sit at the city gates. But the lepers, weakened though they are, marginal and outcasts—never such a healthy lot, come to think about it—are facing the situation and considering what they might do.

One leper says, "Well, it is useless to go back into the city because if we go back into the city, we shall surely die." And the second leper says, "Well, it is useless to stay here by the city gates; what is to be gained by this, by simply waiting?" The third one says, "Then there is only one thing to do and that is to go into the Aramean camp itself, because there, you see, we have a fifty-fifty chance. Either we will be accepted and saved or we shall die. The last lot will be no worse than this one."

It's a very serious decision for any Israelite to make. They must decide to leave the old city, the chosen people. They must decide to go to new territory; they must decide to yield apparently to pagan influences. The writer tells us the lepers went "in darkness."

But a marvelous thing happens. Yahweh goes before the lepers with a great sound, so loud that the attacking enemy believes that somehow or other the Israelites must have been able to hire mercenaries who are coming down upon them, and so they flee the camp leaving the tents full and the table set. By the time the lepers get to the new territory, to what they thought would be the camp of the enemy, they find full tents, an empty camp and, like you tonight, gifts in the wilderness. Then, realizing their responsibilities, they say, "It is not right for us to stay here; our responsibility is to return to the city." In that way the whole community of Israel is liberated, renewed and made effective in the world again.

This siege and these lepers, I believe, are a model of the present development and, as a matter of fact, the traditional development of religious life. Five times in history religious life has been under siege.

It has been under the siege of new needs in Church and society. Each time the response to the siege has been a drastic change in the image, in the basic mode of living religious life so that the religious who followed could go deeper but differently into life, into service, into God.

The desert fathers, for instance—the prototype religious—became solitary ascetics in their society so that they could witness to and maintain a spirit of total commitment in a society where Christianity had become a state religion, where state religions were civic norms and most of the time, therefore, no religion at all.

The desert fathers were the model of religious life from the second to the fifth century, but then there were new needs in Church and society. When the order of the Roman Empire collapsed, the monks joined together and formed stable communities, not as solitary hermits in the desert, but as groups of committed people living together which became the life centers of western Europe from the fifth to the twelfth century. But in the beginning of this new response of religious life they were called lax. Clearly our founder, St. Benedict, was aware of this criticism. At three places in the Rule he points out that we will not be living like those who have gone before us. We lax monks, he says, won't be doing all those things. It took the Benedictines two hundred years to be accepted in the Church.

In the thirteenth century a new set of world forces shaped the Church and society. Cities rose, nationalism raged and mendicant communities developed. These communities said, in essence, that stability was fine, Benedictines, when everybody was on the farm, but it won't work now. Mobility is what is being asked of those who serve the Christ in the kingdom of God. And the mendicants emerged to follow the poor, to serve the poor, to be with the poor. The words of St. Francis record: "I know they will try to make you monastics but don't let them. I am another kind of fool."

At a fourth point in history, when the political power and unity of the Church declined, the apostolic orders rose to defend the Church, the papacy, the dogma, and to make spiritual cohesion the overriding service of religious orders until the eighteenth century. But for these people to serve the Church and the people of God as they needed to be served in that period, founder after founder of the communities represented in this room had to tell their followers,

"Do not call yourself religious or the Church will not let you serve the way we must."

At the fifth point in the cycle, in the nineteenth century, as a period of enlightenment and democracy emerged, teaching congregations rose to do radical things, things which brought fire to the city of Philadelphia and criticism to the Church. Teaching congregations were radical and bold enough to empower the masses, to liberate the poor.

Each of these major images of religious life emerged out of changes—changes in the Church, changes in society. Each one of those images diminished the image before it. Each one of those images was met with official hostility. The world and the Church are changing again, changing even now as we set out this week to begin to articulate a theology of religious life. The Church's definition of itself, the world problematic and a new notion of woman are forming the base of a new world-view. What conclusions can we draw at the beginning of this week?

First, major social or ecclesial changes create new needs. Second, new needs bring changes in the nature—the very nature—of religious life. Third, in the past only those communities survived which were capable of new modes of response. Sixty-six percent of all the religious communities founded before the year 1800 are now extinct. Fourth, religious life, I would submit, is at the gates of the city again, in transition to a new era.

Like the lepers, there are before us three possibilities. We can go back into the city; we can stay where we are—it's getting comfortable; or we can risk moving toward a new vision of religious life, provided we are willing to move in darkness and in uncertainty. For the new vision, like many before it, is in tension with the old. The old vision of religious life says that the purpose of religious life is to be a labor force, to do institutional work. There is a new vision rising that says the purpose of religious life is to be a leaven in society, to be a caring presence, to be nomads who go first where others cannot be.

The old vision of religious life says that religious take vows to keep laws, but a new vision is emerging which signals now that religious take vows to gain life and to give life. The old vision says that the vow enables us to show what we are against; too many things, too dangerous a relationship, too much self. The new vision of religious life says that the purpose of vows is to be for something: to be for the poor, for love and justice, the responsible use of talents, a dynamic relationship with Christ. The new vision of the vows says that vows are creative, not negative.

The old vision of religious life says that religious life is a state of perfection, and that therefore we must be very careful; we must be very correct; we must be very approved. What will the lay people say? The new vision of religious life says that religious life is a search, that it is one state of Christian growth as defined in *Lumen Gentium,* that it is a sign that the Gospel is possible, joyful and other-centered.

The old vision of religious life says that the purpose of religious is to transcend the world, to withdraw, to be private, to be quiet. The new vision of religious life says that the purpose of a religious is to transform the world, like the Christ before her, to be in the world but not of it.

So to be a religious leader in a period of transition or siege is to have to make a leper's choice: to face new questions with only old answers as a guide. Although there are many issues we could talk about tonight—ministry, retirement, community, membership, maintenance—there is only one central challenge, I believe, and that is the challenge of leadership itself. Women who sit in this room tonight have an awesome and immediate responsibility for the future and the very survival of their congregations. I present for your consideration four circumstances which constitute the crises and challenges confronting administrators of religious communities today, as I see them.

First, we must realize that renewal is not over. In fact it may barely have begun. Leaders of the early period of renewal indeed were great, strong women who faced resistance, a high level of emotion, a lot of struggle, a great deal of shock and much criticism. But those women also had high hopes rising across this country. They had a period of great energy. They were supported in their position by a sense of expectation. New leaders—leaders in office tonight, leaders recently elected, leaders who will be chosen six months from now—face the heat of the day. They face the fatigue that goes with long slow efforts. They are tired; their sisters are tired; the parish is tired; the bishop is tired. The people are tired, hot, discouraged, tempted to wonder sometimes if beginning was worth it.

The point I'm trying to make is that, given a trend or a movement in history, given a time and a call and a tide, beginnings are relatively easy. It is going on that's hard. Not settling down, not turning back, not giving up takes courage and leadership. I ask you to remember this week as you make difficult statements that Moses indeed led the chosen people out of Egypt, but Joshua led them into the promised land. If the leaders who follow leaders who began stop, then it's over. Religious communities do not need and perhaps will not be able to survive as caretakers for chosen people. We need leaders who have a capacity for wilderness and the longest, darkest part of the trip.

Second, I believe that we must realize that to be aware is itself to be sent. That is a sign of the sending. I am saying that consciousness is of the essence of prophecy. The realization of the message is what really commissioned every prophet. None of the prophets I know of were called and told, "Be here at the mountain at three tomorrow afternoon, and I'm going to give you a message." They got the message whether they wanted it or not and were told to start.

No prophet—Moses, Jonah, Amos—wanted to criticize the king. All of them argued that they couldn't do it. Others, ones who went before, they said, were better equipped. They all argued that the people would be upset. Paul, too, in Romans 9—10—the most poignant passage of any of his epistles, I think—is full of misery. Paul said, "What happened to the covenant we loved? Where did it go and why did it go?" He loved the old covenant and he loved the Israelites who were clinging to it and he knew that some of them would go on clinging, Christ or not. But his new understanding, his new call and his new vision pressed him beyond it even though in Scripture he describes himself as having "great grief and constant pain."

Third, I think we must accept the fact that the purpose of leadership is not to make the present bearable. The purpose of leadership is to make the future possible. We must remember that many things for which we strive may never be gained in our lifetime. But our debt is not to yesterday. Our debt is not even to today. Our debt is to those who come tomorrow, that they can come in dignity and faith.

So, as we watch one hope and one goal after another be continually unrealized, we must learn to gather strength for the distance ahead from the notion that what may not be for us can be because of us.

Finally, like the Israelites under siege, we cannot now afford to succumb to pressures, to succumb faithlessly in fear. We cannot succumb to the inwardness of our communities. We cannot become reluctant leaders. Reluctant leadership is worse than no leadership at all. Do not state something and then wring your hands for fear it will happen. Of all the religious in this country we are the ones who must go into the wilderness. No, we must lead into a wilderness that is once again taking us deeper and differently into life, into service, into God. We have an obligation, Sisters, to everyone in the city to pursue the new vision with the same kind of commitment, courage, personal discipline and rigorous sacrifice with which we pursued the old. We too have an obligation to go beyond the city gates—to go indeed where there is no trail and leave a path.

15. INTERDEPENDENCE AND REVITALIZATION

W̲e are at Crossroads '76. There is one century closing behind us; we have another one opening before us. It is a glorious moment, heady and very difficult because religious communities are deeply embedded at the present moment in both centuries. They are clinging to one and faced with another, and they are completely devoted to the development of the future, whatever.

There are, in fact, only three other moments in history—the Ice Age, the period of Evolution and the Technological Revolution—and three other centuries—the third, the fifth and the nineteenth—that impacted the human condition as we are being touched at this time. After those moments life was significantly different for everyone. After this moment life will be significantly different for everyone.

Whether we like it or not, we are in the middle of a revolution. The Leadership Conference of Women Religious has been meeting since 1956, only twenty years. Since the leaders of religious women of this country met in national assembly for the first time, the United States has engaged in two wars, both of them a full hemisphere away. Over this period new nations have emerged on the face of the earth. We have conquered space, distance and time.

In other words, the world that so many of us came from, the world that our communities reflect so well, a world that was made up of folk societies—of villages, of little towns, of centralized regions—that were small and isolated and self-sufficient where everyone knew everybody, where no one ever came in, where everything that was needed to exist was made right there, where things were unified and predictable—that world is over. Societies whose people were basically all equal because nothing separated them, because labor was general rather than specialized—everybody farmed, everybody made his own shoes, everybody built his own house—that microscopic world, that world apart from every other world, that independent world is over. We can look at it longingly. We can love it for its richness. We can affirm its strength, but we cannot, even if we would, wish it back.

A Single-City Globe

We are in a post-industrial era. This era has remolded the globe into a single city. It is no longer possible for anybody to say we serve the local church unless we ask: Where is the local church? What is the local church? Twenty percent of the American population moves every year. You cannot teach a child and not influence the entire world. Everything we use for daily existence has been made by resources taken from someplace else in the world.

Seventy-eight per cent of the American population alone lives in cities that are large and fragmented and in a constant state of change. Labor is specialized and the profit system makes people insecure and oppressed. We are living off the labor of every human being in the world. Our world is interdependent now. We are witnessing the dawn of universal history.

The ironic thing is that for all the disparateness and all the fragmentation, we are bonded as we have never been bonded before. The world is bonded by communications, by literacy, by transportation, by technology. The point is that we know about the B-1 bomber. Our great-grandparents would not have. We know about migrant workers. We know about the starving in India. We know about the quality of universal life. We know about the pain in the world village. And we, as members of the Leadership Conference of Religious Women of the United States, can do something about it.

Providing the Experience

The closing of a National Assembly is always a depressing moment. People leave saying, "A great experience. I wonder how you do anything about all that. I certainly wish I could take this home. I wish our Sisters had been here. I wish our bishop had been here. I wish the people back home would have been been here. That's what's hard about being a religious leader." No, Sisters, it is senseless to think about taking this experience home. This experience is our experience. It is not to be taken home. But we can, as religious leaders, provide these same experiences for others. If we decided on only one action this week, it could be to provide these very programs for our own communities so that when other Sisters see and feel and touch the world that we have seen and felt and touched here, they would become one chorus across this land, living and crying justice. That way no one who crosses their path, no civic official can miss the message of the Gospel life because we will bring to it a special quality of presence in the world that is decisive for the kingdom of God.

I therefore wish all of you continuing "dis-ease." If you leave here feeling comfortable, we will know that the assembly has failed. We are in the midst of a new world revolution. We did not create it but we cannot avoid it. We can only deal with it. During this assembly we have been told "to touch the world, to abandon a religion that is simply vertical or only horizontal, to look up and reach out at the same time, to develop a contemplative vision, to do justice, to build something together for the sake of the kingdom of God, to be interdependent." In other words, the moment of truth is now.

There will be no interdependence unless it is first present among us here and now. Even though Sisterhood is indeed powerful and we do love one another (the table conversations have been nice and we know eight more names in the world now), the actual truth is that we are strangers. But no one else is better equipped or more obliged to be interdependent than leaders.

Though at this moment we could clasp our hands around these tables and bind this entire group since it is such a small room for so many of us, the truth is that by tonight we will all be in different parts of the world again. But there is no such thing as interdependence until we as leaders know how to call it forth, and no one but leaders have a better opportunity to model it.

Three Types of Authority

Authority has three types. Authority is expert. There are some people who are so technically expert in certain fields that for anybody else in an elected position to tell them what to do with this television screen or that research project is absurd. There is authority that is moral. There are some figures so charismatic, so central, so demanding of attention that they carry great influence. To step over a dying person in a lobby and let him or her die there is to know nothing about moral authority; to ignore the women in our communities with strong moral influence is to know nothing about moral authority. There is, finally, official authority—authority that is designated by the group and delegatory. It is a function of official leadership, the leadership that is ours, to weld the possibilities of the other kinds of authority into Christian power.

So interdependence is impossible unless we can listen to others and hear them, hear them and be able to take from them. If we have not been able to take from the truth and wisdom of someone else this week, then we have simply had another experience in triumphalism or domination, another model of Western imperialism. There is no such thing as interdependence until we remain constantly touched by someone who is somewhere where we are not. The question today, then, is: Have we as individuals listened to someone else? Have we heard someone else? Have we become part of something bigger than ourselves? Have we been able to bind together some truth that broadens us all? For within each of us is the full power of the Leadership Conference of Women Religious: simple women with great hearts, hard questions and high courage who have broken bread and shared beliefs together this week.

The Leadership Conference of Women Religious has met every year since 1956. For the twentieth time we end a week of national assembly. Some of us have been here often before. For some, it is the first of many times. Whether or not the trip is worth the money it cost our communities to bring us together depends on what the experience means: for each of us personally, for the Sisters whose lives we share at home, for the Church we love, for the people of God whom we serve. This is no simple convention, no professional obligation. It is no vacation. It is, and will be read by others, as a model of Church, a covenant, a public Word. Please God we will speak it loud and clear, for leadership and the on-going life of religious communities are only separate facets of the same pressing issue: revitalization of religious life.

For the past week we have been setting directions together, and this morning we intend to announce the results of those deliberations. Before we do that, however, I would like to take a few moments to consider how new decisions of any kind affect the development of a group.

In May of this year, a popular priest-journalist wrote in his syndicated column that the renewal of religious life in religious communities has failed, that religious life is dead. I do not agree. It is certainly clear that the old order has indeed passed away, but it is equally clear to those who will look inside that something new awaits, is aborning, is coming soon.

The difference between his position and my position revolves entirely around our attitudes toward death. He says that religious life is dead and therefore over. I say that death is of the essence of religious life and therefore life-giving.

The Life Cycle of Institutions

It has become rather basic sociology that institutions, like any living organism, have a life cycle. They go through five phases: the phases of origin, expansion, apogee, decline, and then death or renewal. The period of origin lasts, in arbitrary figures, for about twenty-five years or a generation and is characterized by extensive vision and high risk. It has no traditions, no stereotypes, no roles, no models, no pressures of the past whatsoever under which it labors. Nothing is too much for a young institution: no challenge is too great, no load too heavy, no hope too bizarre. Our foundresses are marked as great according to the degrees to which they were able to depart from the norm. Religious who came to the east coast of this country before the Civil War had managed to cover it with small communities, groups of two or three, before the end of the period of Reconstruction. It was a period of new works, new places, new goals.

In the expansion period, an institution multiplies its accepted activities. In other words, whatever worked for it as it was getting started, whatever is wanted in the society it serves, it does again. It just keeps doing more of the same, and doing it better. The expansion period of an institution is characterized by energy and success—so much success, as a matter of fact, in a given era that the institution

127

finds itself at the point of apogee. It reaches its limits. It develops to the point beyond which it will never develop more in that particular form or fashion. At this stage, the institution standardizes: the rule books get written; things become very, very clear. This period of institutional growth is characterized by effort, uniformity and control.

Then someplace, somehow the world shifts. People need new goods or services, and unless the old institution is prepared to offer them it will begin to decline. It declines when it ceases to respond to new needs either within people, or within the institution itself, or in the society it serves. When people begin to take the poor to the Salvation Army because the switchboard at the convent closes at nine o'clock, the world that our foundresses envisioned has shifted. This period in institutional development is marked by low morale, low productivity and loss of membership. People see no reason to stay.

Reactions to Dying

At this juncture, sociologists say that the institution must renew or die. They say it will be one or the other. They say, furthermore, that renewal is iffy, risky business, fatal to many, and has seen more institutions die than revive. But the sociologist may have run out of steam about death, and the psychiatrist, Elisabeth Kübler-Ross, as a result of her studies on death and dying, may bring to our present condition another dimension to the analysis. Kübler-Ross says that terminally ill patients go through five reactions to the condition:

In the first place the terminally ill simply deny that the illness is terminal, simply deny that this particular condition is serious. Oh, other people have died from it, that's true, but they feel fine; everything is good for them; the whole thing is ridiculous. "Renew what?" we asked.

In the second place, the dying become angry that such a thing would happen to them. Why, when our life and my life was good, would it possibly be taken away? Everything was going so well. I liked things the way they were. How could God dare to interrupt it? God can't want this. "There are important traditions, fine projects in process that cannot be stopped," we said.

In the third phase, the patients bargain. They admit the sickness but they want to control the circumstances. They ask God or their doctors or their families to renegotiate the terms. "If I take the medicine will you let me go back to work? . . . I don't mind being blind, but let me live. . . ." "We have committees, now; what more could they want?" we said.

In the fourth stage, depression sets in. The patient withdraws. Encouragement and reassurance mean very little. The patient feels worthless and very fearful. "It's over," people say. "Religious life is useless; they have ruined it; they have destroyed it."

But the final stage, Kübler-Ross says, is the stage of acceptance. At this point the patient lets go. The patient lets go of past things, is restful, and begins, it seems, to look forward to the new journey ahead.

A New Journey

This Conference has laid out for itself a new journey. We have solemnly pledged to one another to bend our energies and our hearts to five great efforts:

First: To articulate a contemporary theology of religious life consonant with the call to penetrate a dehumanizing culture with the Gospel message.

Second: To effect for ourselves and others an education for justice that leads to systemic change.

Third: To continue study, prayer and action on the woman's issue in collaboration with other groups.

Fourth: To move toward maximum interdependence with other groups and persons to attain our shared goals.

Fifth: To develop a consciousness-raising process regarding our evolving contemporary spirituality.

From Death to Life

A new world is rising. But for new worlds to rise some of the old worlds must die. The passage is painful. But the passage is to life. For we look for the resurrection of the dead, and the life of the world to come. When we were baptized we rose with Jesus Christ. The resurrection is now. And religious are professional futurists, celibates who seek to witness to the eschatological, women who say that of all the things they can do, of all the things they can witness to, they can dictate confidence.

It would be tragic if religious could not die a bit along the way. For we are paschal people. It is important that the world know that of all those blessed and called by God, we are up to at least one summons: going down into the tomb, giving up the spirit and holdings of yesterday. If not, how would we dare to call the rich to give up riches, the oppressors to give up power, when we cannot give up our privileges, our security, our peace. Sisters, this is a new moment, not the last moment.

Let us call ourselves to the third century. Let us promise ourselves to be leaders of the living, for when the history of this period is written we will not be remembered for our hospitals, our schools, our orphanages or our institutions. Our contribution to the history of the Church, if we have the faith to make one, will be religious life itself.

It is a weary time, and we are reluctant pilgrims, but we must remember always another people who were burdened, too, by their blessings. Each time they built the temple, it was destroyed; each time they were more fatigued; each time they called themselves together to build it once again, until finally at the third moment it seemed there was no energy in the group. They had done all they could do. And then Yahweh inspired the prophet and Ezra said, "The Lord God, Yahweh, wants you to know that now is the time to repair and rebuild and revive the city."

Sisters, let us celebrate together the resurrection of the Lord, and our own.